Better Breakfasts

HOME COOKING

© 1994 Time-Life Books B.V.
First published jointly by Time-Life Books B.V. and
Geddes & Grosset Ltd.

Material in this book was first published as part of the
series HEALTHY HOME COOKING.

ISBN 0 7054 2048 5

Printed in Italy.

Better Breakfasts

BY

THE EDITORS OF TIME-LIFE BOOKS

TIME-LIFE/GEDDES & GROSSET

Contents

Better Breakfasts

The first meal of the day has an emotional aura quite unlike that of any other meal. Perhaps this springs from our peculiar vulnerability in the morning, when we still have sleep in our eyes and are feeling a little fuzzy, in need of gentle handling and a shock-free passage from the world of dreams into the world of reality. Presumably we also need nourishment to restore us after our long night's fast. The morning meal, more than lunch or dinner, reminds us of the essential function of food: to fuel our bodies.

When most of us think of breakfast, just a handful of foods and beverages come to mind. These tend to be bland, safe, comfortingly familiar to the point of

being boring: orange juice, grapefruit, bananas or prunes, cereals, eggs, bacon or sausage, toast or rolls, milk, coffee, tea. Added to this are foods typical of particular countries: cheese, bread, ham, boiled eggs in Germany; croissants or bread and jam in France, served with a large cup of *café au lait;* waffles or pancakes and maple syrup in America; and, of course, our own porridge, bacon and eggs, kippers, and toast and marmalade.

In other parts of the world, breakfast is a far more eclectic affair. The Japanese think nothing of having soup upon arising. An Egyptian finds a bowl of beans as appropriate in the morning as in the evening. And a Chinese will happily down steamed or fried rice and a variety of dumplings, known as *dim sum* — 'things that touch the heart'.

Although not all nutritionists believe that breakfast is actually a requirement for a healthy eating style,

they generally agree that the meal is typically a matter of unhealthy extremes. There are many people, of course, who eat literally nothing for hours after arising; they effectively prolong the fast of the night to 12 or 15 hours or even longer. Some adults who follow this pattern get on quite well with their morning's activities. But for children, going without breakfast is another matter. Studies show that children who have had breakfast perform much better in school; they are less listless and can concentrate more effectively on their tasks.

In any case, eating a morning meal appears to make sound biological sense: anthropologists think that our early ancestors were habitual nibblers who, in effect, ate many small meals through the day as they came upon edible berries, fruits or roots. Laboratory studies suggest that people may live longer when they eat three or more meals a day. Experiments with animals indicate that the animals fed one or two large meals gain twice as much body fat as those given the same number of calories divided among more frequent meals. Though the evidence is not clear-cut for humans, many nutritionists believe that eating breakfast does help control weight. Those persons who skip breakfast—or eat very little upon waking—may capitulate to fattening mid-morning snacks or be so ravenous by lunchtime that they overeat.

While most people do not skip breakfast, many eat a breakfast so bereft of nutrition that they need almost not bother. A sweet bun, consumed with a cup of coffee, will be high in calories, fat and sugar, to be sure, but fail to assuage appetite for long. Sugar's simple carbohydrates are quickly absorbed, and instead of a steady flow of energy to keep the body running smoothly through the morning, the level of blood sugar—the form in which energy is supplied to the body's cells—rises sharply to a peak, then declines rapidly, soon to be followed by a gnawing in the pit of the stomach. By contrast, complex carbohydrates are digested slowly, so that they provide a gradual and sustained level of blood sugar that forestalls hunger.

At the opposite extreme is the traditional fried breakfast. With its sausages, bacon, eggs, jams and buttery breads, it is undesirably weighted with cholesterol, sugar and fat, as well as too much protein.

Getting it right

Like lunch and dinner, the good breakfast should strike a balance between the different categories of food. Ideally, about 60 or 65 per cent of breakfast's calories should come from complex carbohydrates, 20 to 25 per cent from fats, another 10 per cent from protein, and the remaining 5 per cent or less from sugar, syrup or honey. Weight for weight, proteins and carbohydrates contain less than half the calories of fat.

Foods that are loaded with complex carbohydrates are said to be nutritionally dense, since they also contain vitamins, minerals and protein. Invariably these foods contain little or no fat. Often the little fat present is of the unsaturated variety that, unlike the saturated fat found in meat, eggs, milk, cream and cheese, has not been implicated in heart disease or other circulatory disorders.

Because they are such a rich source of complex carbohydrates, grains and vegetables are used frequently in the recipes making up this book. You will find these foods served up in tempting variations of traditional dishes, as well as in delicious innovations that can sway the most confirmed breakfast-hater.

Breads of all kinds

No breakfast or brunch would be complete without bread in one form or another—yeast-raised loaves, unleavened flatbreads, muffins, dumplings, buns. Among the breads offered here, some are sweet, some savoury, some baked, others steamed or cooked quickly on a griddle.

For sound health reasons, many of the recipes call for whole grains. Since these have been given only the lightest milling, just enough to strip the inedible outer husk from the kernel, they retain all three edible parts of the kernel: the fibre-rich jacket of bran; the starchy endosperm, which accounts for about 80 per cent of the kernel's weight; and, enclosed by the

endosperm, the germ. It is the germ that gives whole grains their distinctive, rather nutty flavour, as well as their B and E vitamins and protein; the bran supplies the fibre.

Whole grains are marketed in a variety of forms. Groats are the coarsest—they are simply the whole kernel, minus its husk. Buckwheat, oats and wheat (somewhat inaccurately, the wheat groat is called a berry) can be purchased in groat form. Groats are also cracked or sliced into small pieces, or ground into flour or meal of varying degrees of fineness.

Because they retain the oil-laden germ, whole-grain products are much quicker to spoil than more highly refined products. Plain flour will keep up to six months at room temperature. Stored in a tightly covered container in the refrigerator, groats remain fresh for four to five months. The more finely textured products, including cracked wheat, meal and flour, are quicker to spoil. Buy them in small quantities, store them in the refrigerator, and plan to use them within three months.

Several of the breads in this book call for combinations of different flours. Where a light texture is desirable, it is essential to include a large portion of flour milled from wheat. Only wheat contains a significant amount of gluten, the protein that gives bread its structure. Plain white flour produces a lighter-textured bread than wholemeal flour, whose germ and bran content interfere with the gluten's ability to develop fully. Strong white flour has more gluten and creates a sturdier loaf.

Thorough kneading is essential to provide a yeast-leavened dough with good body. But quick breads, which generally are leavened by bicarbonate of soda or baking powder, actually suffer if they are mixed too long or too vigorously. Bicarbonate of soda and baking powder, like yeast organisms, release bubbles of carbon dioxide that cause dough to rise. But whereas yeast tends to work slowly, these agents go into action as soon as they are moistened. Consequently, quick bread batters or doughs should be mixed only long enough to combine the ingredients well—overmixing will drive out the carbon dioxide bubbles.

Do not let a quick bread dough or batter stand for long after mixing, since delaying cooking will allow the carbon dioxide to escape. Once the bread is done, serve it warm or as fresh as possible; it will not benefit from standing around any more than would a griddle cake or a waffle.

Keep your baking powder tightly covered and discard the unused portion no more than 12 months after purchase—otherwise you risk disappointing results. You can test baking powder's efficacy by adding 1 teaspoon to 6 tablespoons of hot water. Few bubbles mean that the baking powder is past its prime.

The quick breads most closely identified with breakfast and brunch are griddle cakes, waffles and French toast. As conventionally prepared, they tend to be high in calories, fat and cholesterol; for this book, they have all been redesigned to fit a healthier mould. Egg yolks have been reduced in the recipes (a single yolk suffices for four people) and egg whites increased, with results that are light, moist and tender. The commercial syrups and spreads ordinarily served with these breads are replaced by homemade versions that are deliberately less sweet, yet full of natural fruit flavour. And fresh fruit is the basis of several delightful toppings.

The fat and calorific content of stove-top breads can be further reduced by the right choice of the pan or griddle. With a non-stick finish or, in the case of a cast-iron utensil, a well-seasoned cooking surface, only a trace of fat need be added to prevent the bread from sticking.

To season a cast-iron pan, cover its cooking surface with a flavourless vegetable oil. Place the pan in a 130°C (250°F or Mark $^1/_2$) oven. After an hour, turn off the heat and leave the pan in the oven for 12 hours. When you remove the pan, wipe it with paper towels to remove any excess oil. To clean the pan after cooking without damaging the seasoning, simply rinse it with water, dry it and wipe it out lightly with a paper towel soaked with a little vegetable oil.

For most people, breakfast is not complete without a bracing cup of hot coffee or tea. Like the frying pan or griddle, the coffee pot deserves special attention. Even if you eschew coffee in favour of tea, cocoa, fruit juice or some other morning beverage, there may be times when you will want to serve a well-made brew. Since bare metal can impart a bitter flavour to coffee, choose a pot made of glass or porcelain and clean it after every use with a solution of bicarbonate of soda and water. (Soap or detergent may leave a residue or film.) And, whether you make coffee by filter, vacuum or percolator method, remove the grounds and serve the coffee immediately or, at the very latest, within half an hour of brewing it. If this is not possible, keep coffee warm over gentle heat; never allow it to boil—boiling will only make it bitter.

How this book works

Time is a key issue. It is the reason that so many people make do with a breakfast that is a skimpy, unsatisfying, rushed affair. With a little planning and organization, however, it is possible to have an appetizing, healthy meal in the morning. For some people, of course, getting organized shortly after rising is not within their nature. Time set aside the night before for a few chores will help speed up operations in the morning. Steps that can be taken in advance are:

• Set the table and get out the utensils you will need.

•Measure and combine all the dry ingredients for stove-top breads, muffins or quick breads; cover them tightly so that no flavours or aromas will escape.

• Mix liquid ingredients for griddle cakes, French toast or waffles; cover the containers tightly and refrigerate them.

• Oil baking tins.

• Cook pancakes, stack them one upon another between pieces of greaseproof paper, wrap them tightly in foil and refrigerate them.

• Prepare frozen dishes such as sorbets or chilled ones such as moulded salads and soups.

• Bake biscuits and yeast breads. Most yeast breads actually benefit from being baked a day in advance, since their flavour will improve and their texture will become firmer, thus making them easier to slice.

• Cook and refrigerate seafood, covered, for use in salads or as filling for pancakes.

• Prepare sauces, toppings and spreads.

• Mix marinades and refrigerate them.

• Cook the base for a soufflé and refrigerate it. The next day, heat it gently before adding the other ingredients.

With some of the work done in advance, you will have more of an opportunity to be with your guests and to enjoy with them a meal that is not only delicious but good for them.

The Key to Better Eating

Home Cooking addresses the concerns of today's weight-conscious, health-minded cooks with recipes that take into account guidelines set by nutritionists. The secret of eating well, of course, has to do with maintaining a balance of foods in the diet. The recipes thus should be used thoughtfully, in the context of a day's eating. To make the choice easier, an analysis is given of nutrients in a single serving. The counts for calories, protein, cholesterol, total fat, saturated fat and sodium are approximate.

Interpreting the chart

The chart below gives dietary guidelines for healthy men, women and children. Recommended figures vary from country to country, but the principles are the same everywhere. Here, the average daily amounts of calories and protein are from a report by the UK Department of Health and Social Security; the maximum advisable daily intake of fat is based on guidelines given by the National Advisory Committee on Nutrition Education (NACNE); those for cholesterol and sodium are based on upper limits suggested by the World Health Organization.

The volumes in the Home Cooking series do not purport to be diet books, nor do they focus on health foods. Rather, they express a common-sense approach to cooking that uses salt, sugar, cream, butter and oil in moderation while employing other ingredients that also provide flavour and satisfaction. The portions themselves are modest in size.

The recipes make few unusual demands. Naturally they call for fresh ingredients, offering substitutes when these are unavailable. (The substitute is not calculated in the nutrient analysis, however.)

Most of the ingredients can be found in any well-stocked supermarket.

Heavy-bottomed pots and pans are recommended to guard against burning whenever a small amount of oil is used and where there is danger of the food adhering to the hot surface, but non-stick pans can be utilized as well. Both safflower oil and virgin olive oil are favoured for sautéing. Safflower oil was chosen because it is the most highly polyunsaturated vegetable fat available in supermarkets, and polyunsaturated fats reduce blood cholesterol; if unobtainable, use sunflower oil, also high in polyunsaturated fats. Virgin olive oil is used because it has a fine fruity flavour lacking in the lesser grade known as "pure". In addition, it is—like all olive oil—high in mono-unsaturated fats, which are thought not to increase blood cholesterol. When virgin olive oil is unavailable, or when its flavour is not essential to the success of the dish, 'pure' may be used.

About cooking times

To help planning, time is taken into account in the recipes. While recognizing that everyone cooks at a different speed and that stoves and ovens differ, approximate "working" and "total" times are provided. Working time stands for the minutes actively spent on preparation; total time includes unattended cooking time, as well as time devoted to marinating, steeping or soaking ingredients. Since the recipes emphasize fresh foods, they may take a bit longer to prepare than 'quick and easy' dishes that call for canned or packaged products, but the difference in flavour, and often in nutrition, should compensate for the little extra time involved.

Recommended Dietary Guidelines

Average Daily Intake		Calories	Protein grams	Cholesterol milligrams	Total fat grams	Saturated fat grams	Sodium milligrams
Females	7-8	1900	47	300	80	32	2000*
	9-11	2050	51	300	77	35	2000
	12-17	2150	53	300	81	36	2000
	18-54	2150	54	300	81	36	2000
	55-74	1900	47	300	72	32	2000
Males	7-8	1980	49	300	80	33	2000
	9-11	2280	57	300	77	38	2000
	12-14	2640	66	300	99	44	2000
	15-17	2880	72	300	108	48	2000
	18-34	2900	72	300	109	48	2000
	35-64	2750	69	300	104	35	2000
	65-74	2400	60	300	91	40	2000

Maximum Daily Intake

* (or 5g salt)

Better Beverages

Almost everywhere in the world, the offering of a drink represents hospitality. The beverage itself, of course, may vary with the climate, the time of day and the customs of the particular country: cooling fruit syrups and sherbets under the hot Middle Eastern sun, a warming brew of tea, milk and yak butter in the rough tents of Himalayan nomads.

As these offerings show, the making of beverages is a colourful and richly varied subject. This volume will teach the reader techniques for preparing everything from a simple cup of tea to a refreshing frappé.

Tea

Tea is one of the best-known of hot beverages and its history goes back more than 1,500 years. Tea plants are known to have been cultivated in China as early as 350 A.D. At first, tea was drunk as a cure for nervous and digestive disorders, but by 500 A.D. it was also being described as a 'pleasing beverage'—although it continued to be valued as a stimulant, particularly by Buddhist monks who found it an invaluable aid to staying awake during their long hours of meditation.

Names such as Pure Delight, the Pearl, and Precious Thunder reflect the esteem which tea enjoyed, and Chinese emperors held epicurean tournaments to appraise new varieties of tea. The making of tea became a stylized ritual, imbued with spiritual and aesthetic symbolism, and the tea was served in exquisite cups specially glazed to enhance the colour of the liquid.

The mystique attached to tea-drinking in China foreshadowed the traditional Japanese tea ceremony, which reached its apogee in the 15th and 16th centuries. This rite took place in a tea-house specially constructed with fragile materials, in order to emphasize the temporality of human life. The building's entrance was low, thus recalling the virtues of humility to those who had to bow down to pass through it—especially to the Samurai warlords, who had to remove their swords.

In the 17th century, the first consignments of tea were brought to Europe by Dutch trading ships, and tea-drinking quickly became a status symbol, especially in England. Here, tea-drinking was not simply a social ritual, but a passion. Dr. Samuel Johnson, the 18th-century English critic and lexicographer, introduces us to 'a hardened and shameless tea-drinker, who has for twenty years diluted his meals with only the infusion of this fascinating plant; whose kettle has scarcely time to cool; who with tea amuses the evening, with tea solaces the midnight, and with tea welcomes the morning.' However, tea remained an expensive luxury until the 19th century, when India and Indonesia began to cultivate tea plants. Then Ceylon (Sri Lanka), Japan, Russia and Africa followed suit, and today tea is commonly drunk all over the world.

All tea plants belong to the *Camellia sinensis* species, which flourishes in tropical and sub-tropical countries. The widely varying characteristics of the finished teas are due to the different soils and climates in which the plants are grown and also the different ways in which the tea is harvested and produced.

The leaves contain natural oils that give the tea flavour, together with caffeine, which acts as a mild stimulant, and tannin, which gives the tea its pungency and colour. Plucking the leaves is a delicate task that is still carried out manually on most plantations, and the best quality tea is made with tender young leaves, especially those that are still unopened.

For black teas, which produce dark liquids with a strong flavour and which are sometimes very pungent, the plucked leaves of the plant are fermented. First, they are spread out thinly and left uncovered to dry—a process known as withering—which makes the leaves pliable and easier to treat evenly. Next, the withered leaves are rolled in a drum; rolling bruises the leaves and breaks open their cells, releasing the essential oils that carry the tea's flavour. The leaves are then spread out again and left uncovered to oxidize. This exposure to air reduces the pungency of the tannin and darkens the colour of the leaves; at the same time, the flavour in the leaves' natural oils develops further. The whole process of fermentation, induced by the enzymes activated during withering, rolling and oxidizing, is stopped by firing the leaves with a blast of hot air. Firing also dries the leaves; drying, in turn, helps to preserve them.

The same process is modified to produce oolong—or semi-fermented—teas, which have a smoother taste and a paler colour than most black varieties. For green or unfermented teas the leaves are steamed to make them pliable, then rolled and fired; because their tannin has not been oxidized, green teas have a pleasantly bitter flavour and yield a very light-coloured liquid.

Coffee

The coffee tree is indigenous to Africa and it was African tribesmen who prepared the first coffee beverage—an alcoholic drink produced by fermenting the juice of ripe coffee berries. Like tea, coffee was first valued mainly for its stimulating properties, and was used for religious and medicinal purposes. Its popularity spread rapidly through the Arab world and, by about 1200 A.D., the Arabs were drying whole coffee berries and boiling them in water to make a hot beverage. About the 13th century, the practice of extracting the beans and roasting them was introduced; and by the 16th century coffee was prepared by pulverizing the roasted beans and combining the powder with boiling water. This method is still widely used today, especially in Middle Eastern countries, and the bitter, pungent drink that results is often known as Turkish coffee.

When coffee was introduced to Europe by the Venetian traders in the 16th century, fanatical priests in Rome attempted to have it banned because of its association with the Muslim infidel. However, before issuing his edict, Pope Clement VIII decided to taste some coffee for himself—whereupon he promptly declared it to be a truly Christian drink.

For more than two centuries, coffee continued to cause controversy. In France, wine merchants objected to the new drink because it affected the sales of wine. In England, coffee-houses— like other public places of refreshment—admitted only men; the women retaliated by publishing a petition complaining that men were never available to help in times of domestic crisis because they were always in the coffee-houses. In Prussia, Frederick the Great objected to the large sums of money that were going into the pockets of foreign coffee merchants; to control the trade, he forbade the roasting of coffee beans to all but a select few and enforced the prohibition with the aid of coffee spies, who patrolled the streets literally sniffing out the offenders. Coffee-houses became meeting places for the disaffected in times of political unrest and so were viewed with hostility by those

in power—though few rulers were as savage as the Ottoman Grand Vizier who punished persistent coffee-drinkers by sewing them in leather bags and dropping them into the Bosphorus.

Until the end of the 17th century, all coffee production remained in the hands of the Arabs and, during the next hundred years, theft, piracy and intrigue were employed in attempts to break the Arabian monopoly. After Dutch spies finally managed to steal seeds from Arabia, plants were cultivated in the Dutch colony of Java and from there were brought to Europe. In 1723 a French naval officer Gabriel Mathieu de Clieu, leading a gang of masked men, abducted the coffee tree in the Botanical Garden in Paris; with this unusual cargo, he set sail for Martinique. Despite having to share his meagre water rations with the tree elude pursuit by pirate vessels and fend off a sabotage attempt by a stowaway Dutch spy, de Clieu planted his tree in Martinique and thus initiated the cultivation of coffee in the West Indies.

Four years later, in 1727, a Brazilian army officer on duty in French Guinea won the heart of the French Governor's wife and persuaded her to give him cuttings from a coffee tree, which he duly smuggled back to Brazil. Since then, Brazil has grown to be the largest coffee supplier in the world today. In the last century, two more species of coffee tree were discovered in Africa—*Coffea robusta* and *Coffea liberica*—but neither matches the flavour of the original *Coffea arabica*.

The coffee fruit, or berry, resembles a cherry in appearance. Inside the berry there are two chambers, each containing an oval bean that is flat on one side. Some berries, however, have a single chamber containing one round bean called a peaberry—from which the highly esteemed peaberry coffee is made. The beans are tightly surrounded by two thin skins. For the finest coffees such as those from Colombia, Costa Rica, Kenya and Mexico the beans are divested of their outer skins, left to ferment and then their inner skins are washed off. On Brazilian plantations both skins are left on while the beans ferment and the skins are milled off after fermentation.

Coffee is classified for sale according to the country—or sometimes the particular region—of its growth. These classifications are indicative only of type; when buying coffee there is no substitute for a reliable merchant and your own experience and palate.

Teas and Coffee

Tea and coffee—those ubiquitous, revivifying beverages—are both very simple to make: the ingredients are brought into contact with hot water so that their flavours are drawn out into the liquid. They are usually served hot, but they need not always be; chilled, they make such cooling summer drinks as iced coffee. Coffee can even be semi-frozen, making a delicious drink with the texture of a water-ice.

The dried leaves of the tea plant are processed in many different ways to make a range of teas, from the strong, astringent Japanese green tea to the full-bodied, smoky lapsang souchong. In addition to tea, many other leaves, flowers and herbs make delicious drinks—they are called tisanes or herbal teas. Tea leaves are bought dried and ready for use; the herbs and flowers for tisanes, however, can easily be dried at home. Both beverages are made simply by pouring boiling water over the dried leaves or flowers, leaving them to infuse, then straining off the liquid for serving.

Coffee is always made from the ground, roasted beans of the coffee tree, but subtle differences of colour and flavour are achieved by varying the way the beans are roasted and the way the drink is made. Roasting develops the flavour and aroma of the beans; they are then ground to allow maximum contact of the solids with the water. Many coffee enthusiasts buy fresh, unroasted beans and prepare them at home.

One method of making coffee works in the same manner as for tea: the ground coffee is steeped in hot water and the liquid is then strained. Another depends on allowing the hot water to drip through the coffee at a controlled rate. Both these methods produce coffee with an excellent aroma and a mellow flavour. A third technique produces a more bitter, astringent drink, by combining the ground coffee with boiling water or even with steam. The taste of coffee is sufficiently assertive to take quite strong flavourings—spices, fruits and spirits, for example—to create sharp and potent after-dinner drinks.

Unroasted beans will keep for four years. Whole roasted beans should be used within a fortnight; once ground, they begin to lose their flavour in a matter of days.

A Guide to Teas

The various methods by which the tea plant (*Camellia sinensis*) can be grown, harvested and treated have resulted in an exciting range of teas with distinct appearances and flavours. The choice includes strong, pungent teas; others that are pale and delicately flavoured; green teas with a refreshing astringency; and scented teas that are perfumed and flavoured with flowers or fruits.

The best-known teas come from India, China and Sri Lanka (formerly Ceylon); but many other varieties are grown in countries as different as Kenya, Japan and the Soviet Union. The most popular teas marketed are blends of two or more varieties, you can, also, of course, blend your own teas at home.

Tea plants are generally grown in cool temperatures, high above sea-level, so that the leaves develop slowly to yield the finest flavour. Teas from the highest territories are usually the most prized.

Fermented, or 'black', teas are those that have been spread out in the heat after harvesting, left for several hours and then subjected to a blast of hot, dry air—a process that concentrates the flavour of the leaves and also darkens their colour. Oolong teas are only semi-fermented— they are exposed to the heat for a shorter time—and generally have a smoother, more delicate taste. Totally unfermented teas are known as 'green': these teas are slightly bitter. The leaves of both green and oolong teas are usually left whole and are tightly rolled. The leaves of black teas—by far the largest category of teas for popular consumption—are sifted and classified according to size.

As well as the range of whole leaf sizes black tea leaves are often broken up to release more of their natural oils. The terms used to describe these leaf sizes are explained on pages 14 and 15; they often form part of a tea's name, for example, 'souchong' in lapsang souchong.

Flavourings to enhance the infusions are largely a matter of taste. Many varieties, especially black teas, can be drunk with milk or a thin slice of lemon. How ever, the flavours of more delicate teas are best appreciated alone.

Black teas: whole leaf grades

ORANGE PEKOE. Long, thin leaves that are closely twisted; yellow leaf tips and bud leaves are sometimes included.

PEKOE. Small, tightly rolled leaves together with some open leaves.

SOVCHONG. The largest and coarsest of the whole leaf grades.

Black teas: broken leaf grades

BROKEN ORANGE PEKOE. Small pieces of leaf and often the yellow tips of the leaves.

BROKEN PEKOE. Slightly larger pieces of leaf than broken orange pekoe.

BROKEN PEKOE SOUCHONG. The largest of the broken leaf grades.

DUST. The smallest of the broken leaf grades, very useful for quick brewing and frequently marketed in sachets.

FANNINGS. Small fragments of broken leaves like dust, useful for quick infusions and most often in sachets.

Teas

ASSAM. A black pungent Indian tea, grown at a low altitiude, yielding a pungent, malty infusion.

CEYLON. A popular black tea yielding a liquid with a mellow nutty flavour.

DARJEELING. A black Indian tea grown in the foothills of the Himalayas, yielding a liquid with a delicate, slightly fruity flavour.

EARL GREY. A blend of black teas from India and China flavoured with oils from the rind of the

bergamot, a small citrus fruit. The flavour of the infusion is aromatic and smoky.

FORMOSA OOLONG. An oolong tea yielding an infusion with a slightly fruity flavour.

GREEN JAPANESE. A green tea producing liquid with a bitter flavour and a pale green colour.

GUNPOWDER. A green tea form China yielding a pale green liquid with a fruity, bitter flavour. Its alarming name derives from the appearance of the rolled leaves.

ICHANG. A black China tea yielding a liquid with a strong flavour, similar to that of Indian teas.

INDONESIAN. A black tea producing a liquid with a mellow flavour; commonly used in blends.

JASMINE. An oolong tea from China, scented with jasmine flowers, yielding an infusion with a light, refreshing flavour.

KEEMUN. A black China tea low in tannin. The infusion has a smooth, mellow taste.

KENYAN. A black tea from Africa producing a liquid with a mild, nutty flavour.

LAPSANG SOUCHONG. A black China tea yielding a liquid with an unusual smoky flavour.

ROSE POUCHANG. An oolong tea, grown in China and Formosa, scented with rose petals.

RUSSIAN. A black tea grown in the Caucasus Mountains. Due to mechanical harvesting, it contains fragments of twigs which give the infusion a distinctive, earthy flavour.

SCENTED ORANGE PEKOE. An oolong China tea made with leaf tips yielding a delicate infusion with a violet-scented bouquet.

YUNNAN. A black tea from China yielding a liquid with a sweet smell and a resin-like taste.

An Everyday Ceremony Carefully Observed

WARMING THE POT.

Heat fresh water in a kettle. Just before the kettle boils, pour a little of the hot water into a teapot; swirl the water around the sides of the teapot and then empty it out. Return the kettle to the heat.

ADDING TEA.

Measure tea leaves— here, Formosa oolong— into the warmed teapot. Quantities for medium strength tea are one heaped teaspoon of leaves for each cup.

ADDING BOILING WATER.

As soon as the water in the kettle comes to a fierce boil pour it into the teapot. Place the lid on the pot and let the leaves infuse—for 5 minutes in the case of tea. You can keep the tea warm by covering it with a tea-cosy.

POURING THE TEA.

Towards the end of the infusion time, stir the tea once, so that it is of even strength. When the tea has infused, pour it into cups through a strainer. Serve it immediately, with a bowl of sugar or honey so that each drinker can sweeten it to taste.

FILLING AN INFUSER.

Place some tea or ti- sane—here, equal pro- portions of rose hips and hibiscus flowers— in the side of the infuser spoon attached to the handle. Close the infuser.

STIRRING THE TEA.

Place the infuser in a cup and pour in freshly boiling water. Allow the tea to in- fuse for 5 minutes. Stir the drink with the infuser, then remove the infuser and serve the beverage.

FLAVOURING WITH CARDA- MOM PODS.

Put cardamom pods and cold water in a pan. Bring the water to the boil, then simmer, cov- ered, for 5 minutes. Take the pan off the heat; let the water in- fuse for 10 minutes. Put black tea and a strip of orange peel in a warmed pot. Return the flavoured water to the boil and pour it, with the cardamom pods, into the pot.

SERVING THE TEA.

Cover the teapot and let the spiced tea infuse for 5 minutes. Stir it once and pour it, through a strainer, into cups. Serve milk and sugar sepa- rately, so that they can be stirred in to taste by each drinker.

A Chilled Variation

STRAINING TEA.

Strain freshly made tea—here, ceylon—into a jug. Sweeten the tea to taste with sugar; add the juice of an orange, lemon or—as here—lime. Stir until all the sugar has dissolved. Let the flavoured tea cool, then cover it and put it in the refrigerator to chill.

SERVING.

Fill a tall glass with ice and wedge between the cubes a few thin slices of the fruit used to flavour the tea—in this case, lime. Pour the chilled tea over the ice up to the rim of each glass.

A Guide to Coffee

Every cup of coffee starts with beans that were grown on a tree. There are many different kinds of coffee, but those with the finest flavour come from the tree known as *Coffea arabica*: these are the beans that are stocked by all good coffee merchants. The Guide on page 18 describes some of the most widely available arabicas. The other main species of bean, the *Coffea robusta*, has a more neutral flavour and its use is generally restricted to commercially prepared blends.

Once they are harvested, the raw, green beans must be roasted to develop their flavour, aroma and colour. Brief roasting gives beans a pale colour and releases a delicate, mild flavour; longer roasting produces medium and dark beans with progressively stronger flavour; the longest roast yields very dark beans that make a beverage with a bitter, pungent edge. As a general rule, if you like milk in your coffee, you should choose the paler roasts; dark-roast coffees are usually best appreciated black.

The roasted beans must be ground. Each coffee-making method requires a specific type of grind. Whenever possible, grind your own coffee immediately before making the drink. But if you buy your coffee ready-ground you should tell your merchant which method you will be using so that the beans can be ground correctly. Unless it is contained in vacuum-sealed packs, always buy ground coffee in very small quantities and store it in a refrigerator or a cool, dark place. Ground coffee begins to lose its flavour within days.

By judicious blending of different varieties of arabica beans, you can create a far greater range of flavours than one variety of bean alone could provide. Mild coffees—such as Colombian, Kenyan and Costa Rican—generally blend well with more assertive varieties, but there are no hard-and-fast rules. With the aid of the Guide and your own palate, you can experiment to create many blends to suit your own taste.

ANGOLAN. The best coffees from Angola are smooth, sweet and fairly neutral in flavour; they make good bases for blends.

BRAZILIAN. Of Brazil's wide range of coffees, the best are the Santos coffees. Bourbon Santos has a sweet, clear, neutral flavour that is good in blends; Parana is harsher but with good acidity; Rio has a harsh pungency and is used mostly for blending with other coffees.

BURUNDI. Coffees from Burundi have a rich, strong flavour and high acidity.

CAMEROON. This West African country produces fine, sweet, mellow arabicas.

COLOMBIAN. All Colombian coffees are rich in flavour, with high acidity, and blend well with other coffees. Medellin has a fragrant aroma; Excelso has a slightly nutty bitterness

COSTA RICAN. High-grown coffees from Costa Rica have a fine, mild flavour, fragrant aroma, and sharp acidity. They are good either drunk on their own, or blended with other coffees.

CUBAN. Coffees from Cuba are sweet and mellow in flavour.

DOMINICAN. The best Dominican coffees are pleasantly sweet and strong, with a full flavour.

ECUADORIAN. Ecuadorian coffees have a sharp, woody flavour that is generally thought to be too dominant served alone; they are best appreciated in blends.

ETHIOPIAN. Wild coffees from the Djimmah and Sidama regions are complex and spicy; they blend well with deeper, richer coffees such as Colombian or Javanese. The cultivated Harar coffees—known as Ethiopian Mochas—have a piquant aroma and a gamey flavour.

GUATEMALAN. These are mild, mellow coffees. High-grown Cobans and Antiguans have a full flavour and a fragrant banquet.

HAITIAN. The best Haitian coffees are sweet, very mellow, rich in flavour and fairly acid.

INDIAN. The bulk of India's coffee comes from Mysore. Mysore coffees have a deep colour and distinctive full, soft flavour that blends well with Mocha. Coffees from Nilgiris are rich and delicately acid.

JAMAICAN. Blue Mountain from Jamaica is ex-

tremely mellow, sweet and aromatic, and its delicate flavour calls for a medium roast.

JAVANESE. The best coffees from Java are rich with a fine acidity. They are best medium or dark roasted and blend well with Mocho, or with Kenyan and Colombian.

KENYAN. These are tart, aromatic coffees with an excellent mild flavour that blends well with other coffees.

KONA. This Hawaiian coffee has a smooth, pungent flavour, slight acidity and fine aroma.

MEXICAN. The best Mexican coffee, Coatepec, is rich and mellow and of fine acidity, with a slight bitterness.

MOCHA. This coffee from the Yemen has a distinctive winy flavour and a high acidity. A favourite for Turkish coffee, it blends especially well with Javanese, Kenyan and Mysore coffees.

NICARAGUAN. These are neutral in flavour, and are most useful in blends.

PAPUA NEW GUINEA. Coffees from Papua New Guinea have a full, smooth flavour.

PERUVIAN. The finest coffees from Peru are delicate in flavour and slightly acid.

PUERTO RICAN. These are sweet, richly flavoured, high quality coffees.

RWANDA. The best coffees, grown on high ground, have high acidity and a rich flavour.

EL SALVADOR. Coffees grown on high ground in . El Salvador have good acidity and a mild flavour. Low grown coffees are slighter, but with a pleasant acidity and a winy taste.

SUMATRA. Mandheling and Ankola are rich, heavy coffees; they are excellent for drinking block. Ayer Bangies is very delicate in flavour.

TANZANIAN. The finest Tanzanian coffee, Kibo Chagga, is rich and mellow, and has a delicate acidity; it blends well with Kenyan.

VENEZUELAN. These are excellent coffees, mild and mellow. The best is Meridas, which has a delicate flavour, without bitterness Caracas is light with a distinctive, pleasant flavour.

ZAIRE. Strongly flavoured coffees are grown in the Kivu and Ituri regions. They blend well with milder coffees.

Roasting Your Own Beans

STIRRING BEANS.

Pour green coffee beans into a heavy frying pan to make a single layer. Over a medium heat, shake the pan, and stir the beans with a wooden spoon, every 2 to 3 minutes. When the beans start to brown, stir continuously. When they are the colour you want, remove the pan from the heat and let the beans cool a little. With your fingers, crack one open: if it is evenly coloured right through, the beans are ready. Use them immediately, and cool them for storage in tightly sealed jars.

Two Ways to Grind Coffee

GRINDING BY HAND.

Adjust the wheels of a hand grinder as desired— the closer the wheels, the finer the grind. Put coffee beans in the bowl, do not fill it to the top lest the beans spill over during grinding. Turn the handle until all of the beans are ground; remove the ground coffee from the drawer in the base.

USING AN ELECTRIC GRINDER.

Fill the top of a grinder with coffee beans. Put on the lid and run the machine for 3 or 4 seconds, then stop it to check progress. Continue to run the grinder until the coffee is ground as finely as you want, shaking the machine every few seconds so that the beans are ground evenly.

Releasing Flavour and Aroma

The wide variety of coffee-making equipment that is available on the market may, at first sight, seem daunting. However, with very few exceptions, all of these devices work by the simple principle of infusion: hot water is combined with ground, roasted coffee beans, and the coffee releases its flavour and aroma to create a mellow, fragrant liquid.

The two methods demonstrated on the opposite page involve steeping the ground coffee in hot water and then straining the infusion; while those on page 23 work by allowing hot water to drip slowly through the ground coffee. The method you choose to make your coffee will depend on personal taste and on convenience.

No matter what method you are using, the basic guidelines for producing a perfect cup of coffee remain the same. Buy the best quality beans you can afford, and either roast them yourself or make sure they are freshly roasted. Whenever possible, grind the beans just before using them: freshly ground beans contribute the richest flavour, and their tantalizing aroma is one of the delights of coffee-making. How finely you grind the beans depends on the method that you intend to use.

The amount of coffee to use depends both on how strong you want your drink and on how finely the beans are ground; fine grinds yield more flavour than coarse ones. As a general rule, use 2 level teaspoons of fine-ground coffee to about 20 cl (7 fl oz) of water, increasing the amount of coffee for coarser grinds.

The best coffee is made with pure water, it should be drawn cold and fresh just before use. To extract the fullest, mellowest flavour, the water should be just below boiling point when poured on to the coffee—about 95°C (203°F); if it were any hotter, the water would also extract the bitter, astringent elements contained in the coffee. To achieve the correct water temperature, allow the water to come barely to the boil, then let it cool for about 10 seconds before using it.

The simplest way to make coffee is to steep the ground beans in hot water in a plain jug and pour the coffee out through a strainer. An alternative method is to use a specially designed pot fitted with a plunger appliance that strains the infused coffee before it is poured out.

An inexpensive way to produce drip coffee is to use a plastic cone lined with a disposable paper filter. The hot water is poured on to the coffee in the cone and left to drip through the paper filter into a cup or jug. The cones and filters are available in different sizes for making different quantities of coffee. Another method is to pour hot water into a pot that is fitted with its own perforated filter section. A slightly more elaborate metal pot enables you to heat the water as well as make the coffee; inverting the appliance causes the heated water to drip through the ground coffee into the bottom of the pot, ready for serving.

The length of infusion varies according to how the coffee is made. When the ground coffee is steeped in hot water, it will take about 5 minutes to release its full flavour and aroma. The coffee must then be strained at once, because longer infusion would make the coffee bitter. Coffee made by any of the drip filter methods is ready as soon as the water has filtered through the ground coffee. If the infused coffee were allowed to stand, it would lose much of its aroma.

Coffee can be sweetened with white or brown sugar, or with honey. It may be drunk black or with cream or milk. Pale roasted, fairly mild coffee beans—such as Brazilian Santos or Guatemalan—combine most happily with milk. Equal quantities of strong coffee and hot milk, mixed together, produce *café au lait*, traditionally served for breakfast in wide, deep bowls.

Coffee beans that are usually darker roasted—Kenyan or Costa Rican beans, for example—make drinks with a pleasantly bitter edge that is best appreciated without milk. Such strong, dark coffee can be given a hint of spiciness by being infused with a pod of cardamom or served with a sprinkling of grated nutmeg or ground cinnamon. A thin strip of citrus rind also makes a refreshing and unusual addition to black coffee.

Steeping in a Jug

PUTTING COFFEE IN THE JUG.

Warm the coffee jug by rinsing it out in hot water. Spoon medium-ground coffee—in this case, Colombian coffee beans ground by hand—into the warmed jug

STIRRING THE COFFEE.

Bring fresh water to the boil. Remove the water from the heat, allow it to go off the boil and then pour it into the coffee jug. To promote on even strength, stir the coffee once with o spoon. Put the lid on the jug and leave the coffee to infuse.

POURING THE COFFEE.

After 5 minutes most of the grounds will have settled on the bottom of the jug and the coffee will be ready for serving. Pour the coffee into cups through a strainer.

Straining Inside the Pot

SPOONING IN COFFEE.

Warm a coffee pot fitted with a plunger attachment. Spoon medium-ground beans—dark roasted Costa Rican are used here—into the warmed pot.

POURING ON WATER.

Heat fresh water to boiling point and remove it from the heat. When the water has gone off the boil, pour it into the pot. Stir the coffee once and set the lid on the pot with the plunger raised. Leave the coffee to infuse.

FILTERING THE COFFEE.

After 5 minutes, press the plunger down gently to the bottom of the pot with the palm of your hand; the filter will trap all the grounds underneath it as it descends.

Trickling Coffee Through Filter Paper

PLACING COFFEE IN THE FILTER.

Fit a paper filter inside a filter cone and set the cone over a coffee pot. Spoon very finely ground coffee—here, Colombian—into the paper-lined cone.

MOISTENING THE COFFEE.

Put fresh water to heat. While it is heating, place the coffee pot on a fireproof mat over a low heat. When the water has barely come to the boil, remove it from the heat and let it go right off the boil. Pour a little hot water over the ground coffee in the cone to moisten it, then leave the coffee to swell for about 30 seconds.

FILLING THE FILTER CONE.

Slowly fill up the filter cone with hot water, pouring it evenly over the coffee. Leave the pot over the heat until all of the liquid has filtered through the cone into the pot. Remove the filter cone, stir the coffee once and serve it immediately.

Filtering Grounds Inside the Pot

ADDING COFFEE.

Remove the lid and the perforated cover from the central filter section of a porcelain drip pot. Stand the pot on a wire rack in a large pan and add enough boiling water to come half way up the sides of the pot. Set the pan over a low heat. Put coarse-ground coffee—in this case, Costa Rican—into the central filter section.

POURING ON HOT WATER.

Replace the filter cover. Pour a little water, at just below boiling point, through the perforated cover on to the coffee in the filter, leave the coffee to swell. After 30 seconds, fill the filter with hot water. As the water drips through, top up the filter with more water as necessary.

STIRRING THE COFFEE.

When all of the water has dripped through into the pot below, lift off the filter section and place it on a saucer to catch any drips. Stir the coffee, put on the lid, remove the pot from the pan and serve the coffee.

Coffee at Full Strength

Coffee made by infusion methods can be strong or weak; you need only vary the proportion of coffee to water. But for a particularly strong and slightly bitter drink, the ground coffee is brought into contact with intense heat to release more of its astringent qualities, as in the techniques shown here.

Espresso coffee is made under the pressure of steam, using fine grounds. Espresso machines vary in design and the manufacturer's instructions should be carefully followed. The machines usually have two outlets to allow you to fill two cups at once; some can be fitted with a filter enabling you to make one cup at a time.

All espresso machines are costly, but they make authentic Italian coffee with an incomparably smooth, creamy texture. The steam they produce also serves to froth and heat milk, which, when poured on top of espresso, transforms it into the delicious, foamy drink known as cappuccino.

Turkish coffee differs markedly from other strong coffees. The coffee is boiled together with the water and the drink is served unstrained. Turkish coffee is traditionally produced in a distinctive pot that narrows towards the top in order to trap the foam that forms on the surface of the liquid. You can, however, use a small pan. Domestic coffee grinders cannot make the pulverized grind required for Turkish coffee: it is necessary to have it prepared by a merchant.

Simultaneous Pouring for Café au Lait

BLENDING COFFEE AND MILK.

Make strong coffee; put it in a warmed jug. In a pan, heat an equal quantity of milk until it just bubbles at the edges of the pan. Put the milk in a warmed jug. Pour the coffee and milk together into a large cup or—as here—a breakfast bowl.

SERVING THE COFFEE.

To prevent the hot milk from forming a skin on the surface of the coffee, serve the drink at once. If you make the coffee by the jug method, you can strain it directly into the cup or bowl while pouring the milk.

Frothing Milk for a Creamy Topping

FROTHING MILK.

Pour cold water into the espresso machine; turn the machine to the highest setting to create steam. Place a jug half-filled with cold milk under the steam pipe. Open the tap of the pipe for steam to escape; move the jug up and down over the pipe, so that the steam froths through the milk.

SERVING CAPPUCCINO.

When the milk is frothy, turn off the machine. Pour the milk at once into large cups half-filled with espresso coffee. If you like, sprinkle a little grated chocolate on top before serving the coffee.

Turkish Coffee, Thick and Sweet

ADDING COFFEE TO SYRUP.

Put sugar to taste and cold water in a small saucepan or—as here— in a Turkish coffee pot. Set the pan or pot over a medium heat. Stir constantly until the sugar has dissolved, then stop stirring and bring the syrup to the boil. Remove the pot from the heat; add pulverized coffee.

BOILING THE COFFEE.

Stir the mixture; return the pot to the heat and bring the coffee to the boil. As soon as froth rises to the surface of the liquid, take the pot off the heat. Let the froth settle, then return the coffee to the heat. Bring the coffee to the boil and let it settle twice more. Remove the pot from the heat.

SERVING THE COFFEE.

Let the grounds settle for the last time, then pour out the coffee into small cups. If you like, serve glasses of water alongside the coffee, so that drinkers can take a sip of water after each sip of the strong coffee.

Laced Coffee with a Blanket of Cream

POURING IN WHISKY.

Prepare a pot of strong coffee according to one of the methods; keep it warm. Put a spoonful of sugar—or more to taste—into a stemmed glass with a wide bowl, then pour Irish Whiskey over the sugar

ADDING THE COFFEE.

Pour the hot coffee into the glass to within about 1 cm (2 inch) of the rim. Stir the ingredients gently until they are blended and the sugar has dissolved.

MAKING A LAYER OF CREAM.

Rest the neck of an inverted dessertspoon on the rim of the glass so that the tip of the spoon's bowl barely touches the surface of the coffee. Gradually pour double cream over the back of the spoon, until there is a layer of cream about 5 mm (¼ inch) thick on top of the coffee.

Apple French Toast

Serves 6

Working (and total) time: about 30 minutes

Calories 315, Protein 10g, Cholesterol 95mg, Total fat 5g,
Saturated fat 2g, Sodium 455mg

1	*loaf (about 500 g/1 lb) unsliced day-old dense white bread, crusts removed*
2	*eggs, plus 2 egg whites*
2 tbsp	*caster sugar*
1/4 tsp	*salt*
1/4 litre	*semi-skimmed milk*
12.5 cl/4 fl oz	*unsweetened apple juice*
1	*orange (optional), peeled and thinly sliced, slices halved*

Apple compote

1	*apple, preferably Granny Smith, peeled, quartered, cored and chopped*
1/4 litre/8 fl oz	*unsweetened apple juice*
12.5 cl/4 fl oz	*fresh orange juice*
6 tbsp	*sugar*
2 tbsp	*currants*
1	*orange, grated rind only*
1/4 tsp	*grated nutmeg*
	pinch of salt
1 tbsp	*cornflour, mixed with 1 tbsp water*

Cut the bread into 12 slices about 1 cm (1/2 inch) thick; cut each slice into four strips. In a large, shallow dish, whisk together the eggs, egg whites, sugar and salt, then whisk in the milk and the apple juice.

Dip the bread strips into the egg-and-milk mixture, turning them once or twice until they are thoroughly soaked with the liquid. Transfer the strips to a large plate or baking sheet as you work. Dribble any liquid left in the dish over the strips.

To make the apple compote, combine the chopped apple, the apple juice, orange juice, sugar, currants, orange rind, nutmeg and salt in a saucepan. Bring the liquid to the boil, reduce the heat to medium low and simmer the compote until the apple is barely tender—about 5 minutes. Remove the pan from the heat and stir in the cornflour mixture. Return the pan to the heat and simmer the compote, stirring, until it is thick and clear—about 1 minute. Transfer the compote to a serving bowl and keep it warm.

Heat a large griddle or frying pan over medium heat until a few drops of cold water dance when sprinkled on the surface. Cook the prepared strips of bread until the undersides are golden—about 3 minutes. Turn the strips over and cook them until the second sides are lightly browned—2 to 3 minutes more. Transfer the French toast strips to a platter and keep them warm while you cook the remaining strips.

Serve the French toast at once, garnished with the orange slices, if you are using them, and accompanied by the apple compote.

Apricot-Orange Breakfast Couscous

Serves 4
Working time: about 5 minutes
Total time: about 10 minutes
Calories 220, Protein 6g, Cholesterol 0mg, Total fat 2g,
Saturated fat 1g, Sodlum 205mg

¹/₄ litre/8 fl oz	*fresh orange juice*
12	*dried apricot halves, thinly sliced*
¹/₄ tsp	*salt*
175 g/6 oz	*couscous*
3 tbsp	*shredded coconut*
	fresh fruit (optional)
	semi-skimmed milk (optional)

Put the orange juice, ¹/₄ litre (8 fl oz) of water, all but 1 tablespoon of the apricots and the salt into a medium saucepan. Bring the mixture to the boil. Stir in the couscous and remove the pan from the heat; cover the pan and let it stand for 5 minutes.

Toast the coconut by putting it in a small, heavy saucepan and cooking it, stirring constantly, until it is lightly browned—about 5 minutes. Spoon the couscous into individual serving bowls. Top each portion with some of the reserved tablespoon of sliced apricot and some coconut. You may garnish the hot cereal with fresh fruit such as raspberries, orange segments, or sliced pineapple or mango. Serve the cereal at once; accompany it with semi-skimmed milk if you like.

Apple Muesli

THE TRADITIONAL SWISS MUESLI, ON WHICH THIS RECIPE IS BASED,
USUALLY CONTAINS DRIED FRUIT, HERE FRESH FRUIT IS USED, AND THE
CEREAL IS MOISTENED WITH BOTH APPLE JUICE AND YOGHURT.

Serves 6
Working (and total) time: about 10 minutes
Calories 160, Protein 5g, Cholesterol 2mg, Total fat 3g,
Saturated fat 0g, Sodium 30mg

1	red apple, quartered, cored and coarsely chopped
1	yellow apple, quartered, cored and coarsely chopped
12.5 cl/4 fl oz	unsweetened apple juice
75 g/2¹/₂ oz	quick-cooking rolled oats
1 tbsp	honey
¹/₄ litre/8 fl oz	plain low-fat yoghurt
2 tbsp	sliced almonds
2 tbsp	raisins
1 tbsp	dark brown sugar

Put the chopped apples into a large bowl. Add the apple juice and toss the apples to moisten them. Stir in the oats and honey, then add the yoghurt, almonds and raisins. Stir to combine the mixture well.

Serve the muesli in individual bowls; sprinkle each serving with ¹/₂ teaspoon of the brown sugar.

EDITOR'S NOTE: If you wish, the muesli can be made ahead and kept in the refrigerator, covered with plastic film, for up to two days.

Banana-Peach Buttermilk Shake

Makes 2 servings
Working time: about 5 minutes
Total time: about 6 hours (includes freezing)
Calories 150, Protein 5g, Cholesterol 5mg, Total fat 2g,
Saturated fat 1g, Sodium 130mg

1 *large banana, sliced*
1 *ripe peach, peeled, halved, stoned and*
sliced
¹/₄ litre/8 fl oz *buttermilk*
4 tbsp *fresh orange juice*
2 *strawberries for garnish (optional)*

Wrap the banana slices in plastic film and freeze them for at least 6 hours. Wrap and freeze the peach slices at the same time.

When you are ready to prepare the shakes, put the banana and peach slices, the buttermilk and orange juice into a food processor or blender, process the mixture until it is smooth—about 1 minute. Pour the purée into tall glasses. If you like, garnish each glass with a strawberry. Serve the shakes at once.

Wheat Berry Bread

Makes 3 loaves
Working time: about 45 minutes
Total time: about 4 hours (includes rising)
Per slice: Calories 105, Protein 4g, Cholesterol 6mg, Total fat 1g, Saturated fat 0g, Sodium 40mg

200 g/7¹/₂ oz	*wheat berries*
1 tbsp	*easy-blend dried yeast*
2 tsp	*caster sugar*
4 tbsp	*dried skimmed milk*
90 g/3 oz	*honey*
90 g/3 oz	*molasses*
45 g/1¹/₂ oz	*wheat germ*
¹/₄ tsp	*salt*
1 to 1.2 kg/2 to 2¹/₂ lb	*strong plain flour*
1	*egg, beaten*
¹/₂ tsp	*coarse salt*

Put the wheat berries and ³/₄ litre (1¹/₄ pints) of water into a saucepan and bring the water to the boil. Reduce the heat and simmer the wheat berries until they are tender—1¹/₂ to 2 hours. Let the wheat berries cool in the cooking liquid, then drain them over a bowl; reserve the liquid.

Combine the yeast, sugar, dried milk, honey, molasses, wheat germ, salt and drained wheat berries with 825 g (30 oz) of the flour in a large bowl. Measure the reserved cooking liquid and add enough water to make ³/₄ litre (1¹/₄ pints) of liquid. Heat the liquid just until it is hot to the touch (43°C/110°F). Pour the hot liquid into the flour mixture and stir them together with a wooden spoon.

Gradually incorporate as much of the remaining flour as needed, working it in with your hands until the dough becomes stiff but not dry. Turn the dough out on to a floured surface and knead the dough until it is smooth and elastic—5 to 10 minutes. Place the dough in a clean, oiled bowl; turn the dough over to coat it with the oil, cover the bowl with a damp towel or plastic film, and let the dough rise in a warm, draught-free place until it is doubled in size—about 45 minutes.

Knock the dough back and divide it into three pieces. Knead one piece of the dough and form it into a ball. Knead and form the remaining two pieces of dough into balls. Put the balls of dough on to a large baking sheet, leaving enough space between the loaves for them to expand. Cover the loaves and let them rise until they are doubled in volume again—about 30 minutes.

About 10 minutes before the end of the rising time, preheat the oven to 180°C (350°F or Mark 4).

Bake the loaves for 25 minutes. Remove the baking sheet from the oven, brush each loaf with some of the beaten egg, then sprinkle each with a little of the coarse salt. Return the loaves to the oven and continue to bake them until they are brown and sound hollow when tapped on the bottom—25 to 30 minutes. Cool to room temperature; each loaf yields 16 slices.

EDITOR'S NOTE: If you plan to store the bread, it is preferable to keep it in the freezer. Refrigeration causes bread to dry out.

Bran Muffins with Dates

Makes 6 muffins
Working time: about 5 minutes
Total time: about 10 minutes
Per muffin: Calories 205, Protein 5g, Cholesterol 2mg,
Total fat 4g, Saturated fat 1g, Sodium 240mg

90 g/3 oz	*stoned dried dates, chopped*
50 g/1¾ oz	*plain flour*
60 g/2 oz	*wholemeal flour*
30 g/1 oz	*wheat bran*
⅛ tsp	*salt*
¾ tsp	*bicarbonate of soda*
¼ litre/8 fl oz	*plain low-fat yoghurt*
90 g/3 oz	*molasses*
4 tsp	*safflower oil*

Mix the dates with 1 teaspoon of the plain flour and reserve them. Combine the remaining plain flour, the wholemeal flour, bran, salt and bicarbonate of soda in a bowl. Add the yoghurt, molasses and oil, and stir gently until all of these ingredients are combined. Fold the dates into the batter.

Line the cups of a microwave deep bun pan with paper cake cases or lightly oil six 12.5 cl (4 fl oz) ramekins. Divide the batter among the cups or ramekins. Cook the muffins on high for about 3 minutes, turning the pan or rearranging the ramekins half way through the cooking time. Test the muffins for doneness every 30 seconds by inserting a wooden toothpick in their centres; when the pick comes out clean, remove the muffins from the oven. Let the muffins stand for 5 minutes before serving them.

Brown Bread with Walnuts and Apricots

Serves 10

Working time: about 15 minutes

Total time: about 30 minutes

Calories 155, Protein 4g, Cholesterol 0mg, Total fat 2g,
Saturated fat 0g, Sodium 160mg

60 g/2 oz	*dried apricots*
12.5 cl/4 fl oz	*buttermilk*
175 g/6 oz	*molasses*
1	*egg white*
125 g/4 oz	*wholemeal flour*
60 g/2 oz	*cornmeal*
2 tbsp	*dark brown sugar*
1/4 tsp	*salt*
1 tsp	*bicarbonate of soda*
30 g/1 oz	*shelled walnuts, chopped*

Put the apricots into a glass measuring jug and pour in 4 tablespoons of water. Microwave the apricots on high for 2 minutes.

In a bowl, mix together the apricots, buttermilk, molasses and egg white. In another bowl, stir together the flour, cornmeal, brown sugar, salt, bicarbonate of soda and walnuts. Stir the flour mixture into the apricots to combine them.

Lightly oil a 23 by 10 cm (9 by 4 inch) glass loaf dish and spoon in the batter. Put a glass pie plate upside down in the microwave oven; set the loaf dish on it. (This is not recommended for ovens with rotating turntables.) Microwave the loaf on medium (50 per cent power) for 8 minutes, rotating the dish a quarter turn every 2 minutes. If areas of the bread start to overcook, shield them with small pieces of aluminium foil. Check the bread to see if it is done by inserting a wooden pick or a skewer into the centre; if it comes out clean, the bread is done. Set the loaf dish on a rack and let the bread cool in the dish for 10 minutes before unmoulding and slicing it.

Buckwheat Crêpes with Mushroom-Tomato Filling

Serves 8 as a main dish
Working time: about 1 hour
Total time: about 2 hours (includes standing time for crêpe batter)
Calories 175, Protein 10g, Cholesterol 45mg, Total fat 6g, Saturated fat 2g, Sodium 225mg

1	egg
35 cl/12 fl oz	semi-skimmed milk
1/2 tsp	caster sugar
1/8 tsp	salt
15 g/1/2 oz	unsalted butter, melted
60 g/2 oz	buckwheat flour
75 g/21/2 oz	plain flour
1/4 tsp	safflower oil

Mushroom-tomato filling

1 tbsp	safflower oil
500 g/1 lb	mushrooms, wiped clean, trimmed and quartered
2	shallots, thinly sliced
1 tbsp	plain flour
12.5 cl/4 fl oz	unsalted brown stock, or 1/4 litre (8 fl oz) unsalted chicken stock reduced by half
4 tbsp	dry vermouth
4	garlic cloves, finely chopped
2	large tomatoes, skinned, seeded and chopped
1 tbsp	Dijon mustard
2 tbsp	chopped parsley
	parsley sprigs, for garnish

Creamy cheese topping

225 g/71/2 oz	low-fat cottage cheese
2 tbsp	buttermilk

Put the egg into a bowl and beat it until it is light and foamy. Whisk in the milk, sugar, salt and butter, and then gradually whisk in the two flours. Cover the bowl and let it stand for 1 hour. (Alternatively, you may refrigerate the batter, covered, overnight.) If the batter has thickened at the end of the refrigeration period, stir in additional milk, 1 tablespoon at a time, until the batter has thinned to its original consistency.

While the batter is resting, make the mushroom-tomato filling. Heat the oil in a heavy frying pan over medium-high heat. Add the mushrooms and shallots and sauté them until the mushrooms begin to exude their liquid—about 5 minutes.

Add the flour to the mushrooms and cook the mixture, stirring, for 1 minute. Add the brown stock or reduced chicken stock, vermouth, garlic and half of the tomatoes; reduce the heat and simmer the mixture for 3 minutes, stirring frequently. Stir in the mustard and chopped parsley and remove the pan from the heat.

When the crêpe batter is ready, heat a 15 cm (6 inch) crêpe pan or non-stick frying pan over medium-high heat. Add the 1/4 teaspoon of oil and spread it over the entire surface with a paper towel. Put about 3 tablespoons of the batter into the hot pan and immediately swirl the pan to coat the bottom with a thin, even layer of batter. Pour any excess batter back into the bowl. Cook the crêpe until the bottom is browned—about 1 minute. Lift the edge with a spatula and turn the crêpe over. Cook the crêpe on the second side until it, too, is browned—15 to 30 seconds. Slide the crêpe on to a plate. Repeat the process with the remaining batter, brushing the pan lightly with more oil if the crêpes begin to stick. Stack the cooked crêpes on the plate as you go. Cover the crêpes with a towel and set them aside. There should be about 16 crêpes.

Preheat the oven to 180°C (350°F or Mark 4). Spoon 2 tablespoons of the filling down the centre of a crêpe. Roll the crêpe to enclose the filling, then transfer it to a lightly oiled shallow baking dish. Continue filling and rolling the remaining crêpes, transferring them to the baking dish as you work. Bake the filled crêpes for 15 minutes.

While the crêpes are baking, make the cheese topping. Put the cottage cheese into a food processor or a blender and purée it. Add the buttermilk and process the mixture until it is blended.

Garnish the crêpes with the remaining chopped tomato and the parsley sprigs and serve them with the cheese topping.

Granola

WITH MILK ADDED, THIS GRANOLA BECOMES A BREAKFAST IN ITSELF.

Serves 8

Working (and total) time: about 30 minutes

Calories 255, Protein 6g, Cholesterol 0mg, Total fat 10g,
Saturated fat 1g, Sodium 100mg

75 g/2^1/2 oz	rolled oats
25 g/^{3}/4 oz	wheat bran
30 g/1 oz	untoasted sunflower seeds
60 g/2 oz	whole blanched almonds
2 tbsp	sesame seeds
2 tsp	safflower oil
^{1}/4 tsp	salt
150 g/5 oz	raisins
10	dates, stoned and chopped
2 tbsp	honey
1 tsp	pure vanilla extract
1	orange, grated rind only

Preheat the oven to 200°C (400°F or Mark 6). Combine the oats, bran, sunflower seeds, almonds, sesame seeds, oil and salt in a large bowl. Spread the mixture evenly on a baking tray and toast it in the oven, stirring the mixture every 5 minutes, until it is lightly browned—about 15 minutes.

Return the toasted mixture to the bowl. Stir in the raisins, dates, honey, vanilla extract and orange rind. Let the granola cool completely before storing it in an airtight container. Serve the granola in individual bowls, with semi-skimmed milk poured over it if you like.

Basic Bagels

Makes 12 bagels
Working time: about 1 hour
Total time: about 1 hour and 30 minutes
Per bagel: Calories 135, Protein 5g, Cholesterol 0mg,
Total fat 1g, Saturated fat 0g, Sodium 95mg

15 g/^{1}/$_2$ oz	*easy-blend dried yeast*
4 tbsp	*caster sugar*
^{1}/$_2$ tsp	*salt*
300 g/10 oz	*plain flour*
175 g/6 oz	*wholemeal flour*
30 g/1 oz	*cornmeal*
1	*egg white, beaten with 2 tbsp water*
2 tbsp	*caraway seeds, sesame seeds or poppy seeds, or ^{1}/$_2$ small onion, finely chopped (optional)*

In a large bowl, stir together the yeast, 2 tablespoons of the sugar, the salt, the plain flour and 60 g (2 oz) of the wholemeal flour. In a small saucepan, heat 35 cl (12 fl oz) of water just until it is hot to the touch (43°C/110°F). Pour the water into the yeast-flour mixture and mix the dough thoroughly with a wooden spoon; the dough will be very soft. Gradually stir in enough of the remaining wholemeal flour to form a stiff dough.

Turn the dough out on to a floured surface and knead it until it is smooth and elastic—about 5 minutes. Transfer the dough to a lightly oiled large bowl and turn the dough over to coat it with the oil. Cover the bowl with a damp towel or plastic film and place it in a warm, draught-free place. Let the dough rise until it has doubled in bulk—15 to 20 minutes.

Meanwhile, pour 3 litres (5 pints) of water into a large pan, add the remaining 2 tablespoons of sugar and heat the water until it is simmering. Preheat the oven to 230°C (450°F or Mark 8). Lightly butter a baking sheet and then sprinkle it with the cornmeal; set the baking sheet aside. If you plan to top the bagels with the chopped onion, lightly oil a small, non-stick frying pan and sauté the onion until it is lightly browned.

Transfer the risen dough to a floured surface. Knock the dough back and then divide it into 12 pieces. Form each piece into a neat ball, rolling it around between the palms of your hands until it is smooth. To form rings, poke a floured finger through the centre of each ball and move your finger in a circle to widen the hole until it is about 5 cm (2 inches) in diameter. Place the bagels on the work surface, cover them with a towel or plastic film and let them rise until they are slightly larger—about 5 minutes.

With a slotted spoon, carefully put three or four bagels into the simmering water. Poach them for 30 seconds, turn them over, and poach them for 30 seconds more. Lift out the bagels and set them on a kitchen towel to drain. Repeat the process with the remaining bagels. When all of the bagels have been poached and drained, transfer them to the prepared baking sheet. Brush the bagels with the beaten egg white and, if you like, sprinkle them with some of the caraway, sesame or poppy seeds, or the sautéed onion.

Bake the bagels until they are well browned about 25 minutes. Transfer them to a rack to cool. If you like, serve them with the savoury vegetable spread and the smoked salmon spread.

Variations
Rye Bagels

Substitute 350 to 375 g (12 to 13 oz) of strong plain flour and 100 g (3^1/$_2$ oz) of rye flour for the flours in the basic recipe.

Combine the yeast, 2 tablespoons of the sugar, the salt, the rye flour and 250 g (8 oz) of the plain flour in a large bowl. Pour in the hot water, as described, and mix the dough thoroughly. Add enough of the remaining plain flour to form a stiff dough, then proceed with the basic bagel recipe.

Wholemeal and Oat Bran Bagels

Substitute 425 g (15 oz) of strong plain flour, 30 g (1 oz) of oat bran and 30 to 60 g (1 to 2 oz) of wholemeal flour for the flours in the basic recipe.

Combine the yeast, 2 tablespoons of the sugar, the salt, two thirds of the plain flour and the oat bran in a large bowl. Pour in the hot water, as described, and mix the dough thoroughly. Add the remaining plain flour and enough of the wholemeal flour to make a stiff dough, then proceed with the basic bagel recipe.

Filled Wholemeal Monkey Bread

THIS IS A REDUCED-FAT VERSION OF MONKEY BREAD, BALLS OF SWEET
YEAST DOUGH BAKED IN A TUBE CAKE TIN.

Serves 8

Working time: about 30 minutes

Total time: about 2 hours and 30 minutes (includes rising)

Calories 350, Protein 7g, Cholesterol 10mg, Total fat 7g,
Saturated fat 3g, Sodium 155mg

300 g/10 oz	*strong plain flour*
125 g/4 oz	*wholemeal flour*
110 g/3³/₄ oz	*caster sugar*
¹/₂ tsp	*salt*
1 tbsp	*easy-blend dried yeast*
¹/₄ litre/8 fl oz	*semi-skimmed milk*
4 tbsp	*seedless raisins*
4 tbsp	*sultanas or chopped dried apricots*
4 tbsp	*chopped walnuts*
1 tsp	*unsweetened cocoa powder*
4 tbsp	*dark brown sugar*
2 tbsp	*honey*
1¹/₂ tsp	*ground cinnamon*
30 g/1 oz	*unsalted butter, melted*

To make the bread dough, mix the plain flour, the
wholemeal flour, 1 tablespoon of the caster sugar, the
salt and the yeast together in a large bowl and make a
well in the centre of the dry ingredients. In a small
saucepan, heat the milk just until it is hot to the touch
(43°C/110°F). Stir the hot liquid into the flour mixture.

Turn the dough out on to a floured surface and
knead the dough until it is smooth and elastic—about
10 minutes. Put it into a large bowl, cover the bowl,
and let the dough rise in a warm place until it has doubled in bulk—about 45 minutes.

For the filling, combine the raisins, sultanas or apricots, walnuts, cocoa powder, brown sugar, honey
and ¹/₂ teaspoon of the cinnamon in a bowl. In another
bowl, combine the remaining caster sugar and the remaining cinnamon. Set the bowls aside.

Knock the dough back and turn it out on to a lightly
floured surface. Form the dough into a log shape and
cut the dough into 16 pieces. Flatten the pieces into
10 cm (4 inch) rounds.

Put about 2 tablespoons of the filling in the middle
of each dough round and form a ball (*below*). Lightly
dip the ball into the melted butter, then roll it in the
cinnamon-sugar mixture. Repeat this process with
the remaining dough rounds and filling. Arrange the
balls in a non-stick or lightly oiled 2 litre (3¹/₂ pint) ca-
pacity tube cake tin or savarin mould with the pinched
edges of the balls towards the inside. Cover the pan
and let the dough rise until it has again doubled in
bulk—about 30 minutes. Meanwhile, preheat the
oven to 190°C (375°F or Mark 5).

Bake the bread until it is browned and sounds hollow when tapped—35 to 45 minutes. Put a serving
plate on top of the pan and turn both over to invert the
bread on to the plate. Serve the monkey bread warm.

Preparing Monkey Bread

*1 FILLING AND FORMING A
BALL.*

After placing about 2 tablespoons
of filling on to the middle of a
dough round (recipe, above),
gather up the sides of the round
with your fingers. Pinch the rim
together firmly to seal the filling
inside.

2 COATING THE BALL.

Dip the ball into the small container of melted butter. Then roll
the ball in the prepared cinnamon-
sugar mixture until it is completely coated.

3 ARRANGING THE BREAD.

Put the ball into a non-stick or
lightly oiled 2 litre (3¹/₂ pint) tube
cake tin, with the pinched edge
facing the hole of the tin. Fill,
form and place the other balls in
the same manner, packing them
into the tin side by side. Cover the
tin and bake as directed in the
recipe.

Cardamom Muffins

Makes 12 muffins
Working time: about 15 minutes
Total time: about 40 minutes
Per muffin: Calories 195, Protein 4g, Cholesterol 6mg,
Total fat 6g, Saturated fat 2g, Sodium 145mg

30 g/1 oz	*shelled walnuts*
225 g/7¹/₂ oz	*plain flour*
150 g/5 oz	*caster sugar*
¹/₂ tsp	*ground cinnamon*
¹/₂ tsp	*baking powder*
¹/₄ tsp	*salt*
30 g/1 oz	*unsalted butter, cut into pieces and chilled*
30 g/1 oz	*unsalted polyunsaturated margarine, cut into pieces and chilled*
1 tsp	*ground cardamom or allspice*
125 g/4 oz	*wholemeal flour*
¹/₂ tsp	*bicarbonate of soda*
30 cl/¹/₂ pint	*buttermilk*
1 tsp	*pure vanilla extract*

Preheat the oven to 190°C (375°F or Mark 5). Lightly oil 12 cups of a deep bun tin.

In a small baking tin, toast the walnuts in the oven until they are fragrant and slightly darker—about 10 minutes. Set the toasted nuts aside to cool.

In a bowl, combine the plain flour, sugar, cinnamon, baking powder and salt. Using a pastry blender or two knives, cut in the butter and margarine until the mixture resembles coarse meal. Transfer 4 tablespoons of the mixture to a food processor; add the cardamom and the toasted walnuts and process to fine crumbs; this will be used as a topping for the muffins. Set the topping aside.

Add the wholemeal flour and the bicarbonate of soda to the remaining flour mixture and mix them in well. Pour in the buttermilk and vanilla extract, and stir the ingredients just until they are blended; do not overmix.

Spoon the batter into the cups in the bun tin, filling each one about half full. Sprinkle the muffins with the crumb topping. Bake the muffins until they are well browned and firm to the touch—20 to 25 minutes.

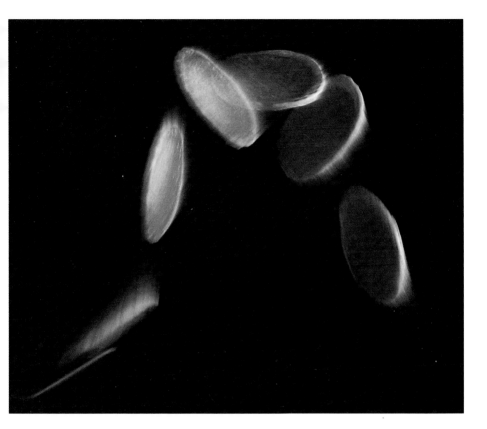

Cornmeal Buttermilk Pancakes

Serves 6
Working (and total) time: about 20 minutes
Calories 285, Protein 8g, Cholesterol 95mg, Total fat 7g,
Saturated fat 1g, Sodium 245mg

175 g/6 oz *plain flour*
3 tbsp *caster sugar*
1/2 tsp *bicarbonate of soda*
1/4 tsp *salt*
125 g/4 oz *cornmeal*
2 *eggs*
35 cl/12 fl oz *buttermilk*
2 tbsp *safflower oil*

Sift the flour, sugar, bicarbonate of soda and salt into a bowl; stir in the cornmeal. In another bowl whisk together the eggs, buttermilk and oil.

Pour the buttermilk mixture into the dry ingredients and whisk them quickly together until they are just blended; do not overmix.

Heat a large griddle or frying pan over medium heat until a few drops of cold water dance when sprinkled on the surface. Drop 2 tablespoons of the batter on to the hot griddle or pan, and use the back of the spoon to spread the batter into a round. Fill the pan with pancakes; cook them until the tops are covered with bubbles and the undersides are golden—1 to 2 minutes. Flip the pancakes over and cook them until the second sides are lightly browned—about 1 minute more. Transfer the pancakes to a platter and keep them warm while you cook the remaining batter.

Serve the pancakes immediately, accompanied by a topping of your choice.

Blueberry Syrup

Makes about 90 cl (1½ pints)
Working (and total) time: about 15 minutes
Per 3 tablespoons: Calories 55, Protein 0g, Cholesterol
0mg, Total fat 0g, Saturated fat 0g, Sodium 1mg

300 g/10 oz *fresh blueberries or blackcurrants picked
over and stemmed, or frozen blueberries
or blackcurrants*
200 g/7 oz *sugar*
1 *lemon, rind julienned and juice reserved*
1 *orange, rind julienned and juice reserved*
1 tbsp *cornflour, mixed with 1 tbsp water*

Combine ¼ litre (8 fl oz) of water, the blueberries or blackcurrants, sugar, lemon rind and lemon juice, and orange rind and orange juice in a saucepan; bring the mixture to the boil. Reduce the heat to medium low and simmer the berries, stirring, for 1 minute.

Remove the saucepan from the heat and stir in the cornflour mixture. Return the pan to the heat and simmer the syrup until it becomes thick and clear—about 1 minute more.

Gingerbread Waffles

Serves 6

Working (and total) time: about 30 minutes

Calories 355, Protein 11g, Cholesterol 50mg, Total fat 7g,
Saturated fat 1g, Sodium 315mg

150 g/5 oz	*plain flour*
125 g/4 oz	*wholemeal flour*
100 g/3¹/₂ oz	*caster sugar*
1 tsp	*ground cinnamon*
1 tsp	*ground ginger*
1 tsp	*dry mustard*
¹/₂ tsp	*bicarbonate of soda*
¹/₂ tsp	*baking powder*
¹/₄ tsp	*ground cloves*
¹/₄ tsp	*salt*
30 cl/¹/₂ pint	*buttermilk*
1	*egg, separated, plus 1 egg white*
90 g/3 oz	*dark molasses*
2 tbsp	*safflower oil*
1	*lemon, rind only, julienned*
Lemon-yoghurt topping	
¹/₄ litre/8 fl oz	*plain low-fat yoghurt*
1 tbsp	*fresh lemon juice*
1	*egg white*
2 tbsp	*caster sugar*

To make the topping, combine the yoghurt and lemon juice in a bowl. Beat the egg white with the sugar in another bowl until soft peaks form. Fold the beaten egg white into the yoghurt mixture. Set the topping aside while you make the waffles.

Combine the flours, sugar, cinnamon, ginger, mustard, bicarbonate of soda, baking powder, cloves and salt in a bowl. In another bowl, whisk together the buttermilk, egg yolk, molasses and oil; pour this mixture into the dry ingredients. Stir the batter until the ingredients are just blended; do not overmix.

Beat the two egg whites until they form soft peaks. Gently fold them into the batter. Prepare the waffle iron according to the manufacturer's instructions. Ladle enough of the batter on to the preheated surface of the grid to cover it by two thirds. Close the lid and bake the waffle until steam no longer escapes from the sides of the iron and the waffle is crisp and golden—3 to 5 minutes. Continue making waffles in the same manner until all of the batter is used. Although these waffles are best served immediately, you may transfer them to an ovenproof plate as you make them, and keep them warm in a 100°C (200°F or Mark ¹/₄) oven until all are ready.

Garnish the waffles with some of the lemon rind and serve them with the lemon-yoghurt topping.

Hot and Spicy Tomato Juice

Makes 4 servings
Working time: about 10 minutes
Total time: about 20 minutes
Calories 40, Protein 2g, Cholesterol 0mg, Total fat 0g,
Saturated fat 0g, Sodium 18mg

800 g/1³/₄ lb	*canned whole tomatoes, puréed in a food processor or a blender and sieved*
3 tbsp	*fresh lime juice*
¹/₈ tsp	*ground cayenne pepper*
2 tbsp	*chopped fresh mint*
4	*lime slices, for garnish (optional)*

Combine the puréed tomatoes, lime juice, cayenne pepper and mint in a non-reactive saucepan. Heat the mixture over low heat and simmer it for 10 minutes. Garnish each serving with a slice of lime, if you like, and serve the drink hot.

Lean Beef Sausages

Serves 4 as a main dish
Working time: about 20 minutes
Total time: about 40 minutes
Calories 100, Protein 14g, Cholesterol 35mg, Total fat 4g,
Saturated fat 1g, Sodium 125mg

250 g/8 oz	*beef topside, trimmed of fat and minced*
2.5 cl/4 fl oz	*unsalted brown stock*
2 tbsp	*fresh breadcrumbs*
1/2 tsp	*grated lemon rind*
1/2 tsp	*finely chopped garlic*
1 tsp	*chopped fresh sage, or 1/4 tsp crumbled dried sage*
1/2 tsp	*paprika*
1	*egg white*
1/8 tsp	*salt*
	freshly ground black pepper

In a large bowl, mix together the beef, brown stock, breadcrumbs, lemon rind, garlic, sage, paprika, egg white, salt and some pepper.

Arrange half of the beef mixture in a line on a piece of strong aluminium foil about 30 cm (12 inches) long. Form one sausage following the technique shown opposite. Using the remaining meat mixture, shape a second sausage.

Pour enough water into a large pan to fill it about 2.5 cm (1 inch) deep. Set a vegetable steamer in the pan and put the sausages into it. Cover the pan and bring the water to the boil. Steam the sausages until they are firm—7 to 10 minutes. Remove the steamer from the pan and let the sausages cool in the foil. Remove the foil from the sausages and cut them in half crosswise.

Heat a non-stick frying pan over medium-high heat, put the sausages into the pan and cook them until they are well browned on all sides—4 to 5 minutes in all. Serve the sausages at once.

Irish Soda Scones with Currants and Caraway Seeds

Makes 24 scones
Working time: about 15 minutes
Total time: about 30 minutes
Per scone: Calories 85, Protein 2g, Cholesterol 13mg, Total fat
2g, Saturated fat 1g, Sodium 120mg

300 g/10 oz	*plain flour*
125 g/4 oz	*wholemeal flour*
2 tbsp	*caster sugar*
2 tsp	*baking powder*
1 tsp	*bicarbonate of soda*
1/4 tsp	*salt*
30 g/1 oz	*cold unsalted polyunsaturated margarine*
15 g/1/2 oz	*cold unsalted butter*
1 tbsp	*caraway seeds*
1	*egg*
1/4 litre/8 fl oz	*buttermilk*
75 g/21/2 oz	*currants*
2 tbsp	*semi-skimmed milk*

Preheat the oven to 180°C (350°F or Mark 4). In a bowl, combine the two flours, the sugar, baking powder, bicarbonate of soda and salt. Using a pastry blender or two knives, cut in the margarine and butter until the mixture resembles coarse meal. In another bowl, whisk the caraway seeds, egg and buttermilk together. Stir the buttermilk mixture and the currants into the flour mixture. (The dough will become too stiff to stir before all the flour is mixed in.)

Turn the dough out on to a lightly floured surface and knead it gently just until the flour is incorporated. Roll or pat the dough so that it is about 2 cm (3/4 inch) thick. Cut out rounds with a 5 cm (2 inch) biscuit cutter or the rim of a small glass, and place the scones on an ungreased baking sheet. Gather up the scraps of dough, form them into a ball, and repeat the process. Brush the scones with the milk and cut a cross on the top of each with the tip of a sharp knife or a pair of scissors. Bake the scones until they are golden-brown—about 15 minutes. Serve the scones while they are hot.

Mixed Vegetable Eye Opener

Makes 2 servings
Working time: about 20 minutes
Total time: about 1 hour (includes chilling)
Calories 65, Protein 3g, Cholesterol 0mg, Total fat 0g,
Saturated fat 0g, Sodium 210mg

2	sticks celery, trimmed, leaves reserved
1	small cucumber, peeled, seeded and coarsely chopped
1½ tsp	fresh lemon juice
8	drops Tabasco sauce
400 g/14 oz	canned whole tomatoes, seeded with their juice
⅛ tsp	salt
½ tsp	caster sugar
2	spring onions, white parts only, coarsely chopped
½ tsp	ground ginger
¼ tsp	dill seeds (optional)
1	carrot, quartered lengthwise, for garnish

Remove the strings from the celery using a vegetable peeler or a paring knife. Cut the sticks into 2.5 cm (1 inch) pieces and set them aside.

Place the cucumber, lemon juice and Tabasco sauce in a food processor or a blender; process the mixture until it is smooth. Add the celery pieces and purée the mixture. Add the tomatoes and their juice, the salt, sugar, spring onions, ginger and ⅛ teaspoon of the dill seeds, if you are including them, and process the mixture, until it is smooth again.

Chill the mixture for at least 40 minutes. Pour the drink into glasses; sprinkle each serving with a few of the remaining dill seeds if you are using them, then float the reserved celery leaves on top. Insert one or two carrot sticks into each drink and serve.

EDITOR'S NOTE: To frost the glasses, place them in the freezer for 30 minutes before serving the drink.

Multigrain Cereal Mix

This uncooked cereal can be as varied or simple as you like. You may leave out one or two of the grains. Most of the ingredients are readily found in the supermarket. The millet and brown rice flakes are found in most health food stores.

Makes about 16 servings
Working (and total) time: about 10 minutes
Calories 100, Protein 2g, Cholesterol 0mg, Total fat 1g, Saturated fat 0g, Sodium 25mg

75 g/2¹/₂ oz	rolled oats
15 g/¹/₂ oz	puffed wheat
75 g/2¹/₂ oz	millet flakes
100 g/3¹/₂ oz	brown rice flakes
100 g/3¹/₂ oz	wheat flakes
60 g/2 oz	sultanas
2 tbsp	chopped toasted hazelnuts

Combine the cereals in a large bowl. Stir in the sultanas and the chopped nuts.

Store the cereal mix in an airtight container. If you wish, serve each portion with semi-skimmed milk or low-fat yoghurt.

EDITOR'S NOTE: You may add 45 g (1¹/₂ oz) of chopped, stoned dates or 1 tablespoon of toasted sunflower seeds to this cereal. To toast the nuts or sunflower seeds, put them in a heavy frying pan over medium-high heat and stir them constantly until they are lightly browned—2 to 3 minutes.

49

Orange and Banana Porridge

Serves 4

Calories 195, Protein 6g, Cholesterol 1mg, Total fat 2g,
Saturated fat 0g, Sodium 17mg

33 cl/11 fl oz *fresh orange juice*
1 tsp *grated orange rind*
1 *banana, coarsely chopped*
125 g/4 oz *quick-cooking rolled oats*
12.5 cl/4 fl oz *skimmed milk*
1 *orange, peeled and segmented*

Combine the orange juice, orange rind and banana in a non-reactive saucepan and bring the mixture to the boil. Stir in the rolled oats, reduce the heat to low and cook the mixture, covered, for 1 minute. Take the pan from the heat and let the porridge stand, covered, until it has thickened—about 1 minute more.

Spoon the cereal into four individual bowls; add 2 tablespoons of the milk to each bowl and garnish with one or two of the orange segments. Serve the porridge at once.

Orange Slices
with Pomegranate Seeds

Serves 6

Working time: about 15 minutes
Total time: about 45 minutes (includes chilling)
Calories 75, Protein 1g, Cholesterol 0mg, Total fat 1g,
Saturated fat 0g, Sodium 3mg

3	*oranges*
1¹/₂ tbsp	*finely chopped crystallized ginger*
12.5 cl/4 fl oz	*fresh orange juice*
1 tbsp	*dark rum*
2 tbsp	*sugar*
¹/₂ tsp	*pure vanilla extract*
4 tbsp	*fresh pomegranate seeds, or one kiwi fruit, peeled, quartered and thinly sliced*

Using a sharp, stainless steel knife, cut off both ends of one of the oranges. Stand the orange on end and

cut away vertical strips of the peel and pith. Slice the orange into 5 mm (¹/₄ inch) thick rounds. Peel and slice the remaining oranges the same way.

Sprinkle the ginger into the bottom of a 22 cm (9 inch) non-reactive pie plate. Arrange the orange slices in a spiral pattern, overlapping them slightly, and set the pie plate aside.

Combine the orange juice, rum and sugar in a small non-reactive saucepan over medium-high heat and boil the mixture for 5 minutes. Remove the pan from the heat and let the syrup cool slightly, then stir in the vanilla extract. Pour the syrup over the orange slices and chill the fruit thoroughly.

Invert a serving plate over the pie plate, quickly turn both over together, and lift away the pie plate. Sprinkle the orange slices with the pomegranate seeds, or scatter the kiwi fruit over the oranges, and serve at once.

Plaited Brioche Loaf

Makes 26 slices
Working time: about 20 minutes with a mixer, 30 minutes
by hand
Total time: about 8 hours (includes rising)
Per slice: Calories 100, Protein 3g, Cholesterol 20mg,
Total fat 3g, Saturated fat 1g, Sodium 45mg

500 g/1 lb	*strong plain flour*
1/4 tsp	*salt*
1 1/3 tbsp	*caster sugar*
20 g/3/4 oz	*fresh yeast, or 15 g (1/2 oz) dried yeast*
2	*eggs*
3	*egg whites*
60 g/2 oz	*unsalted butter, softened*
1 tsp	*skimmed milk*

Sift the flour, salt and 1 tablespoon of the sugar into
the bowl of an electric mixer—or directly on to the
work surface, if you are making the brioche by hand.
Make a well in the centre.

Dissolve the fresh yeast in 4 tablespoons of tepid
water, or reconstitute the dried yeast according to the
manufacturer's instructions. Lightly whisk the eggs
and egg whites together. Pour the yeast and eggs
into the flour well. Using a dough hook on the mixer,
mix on slow speed for 1 minute, then on medium
speed for 2 minutes, or until the dough is no longer
sticky. Gradually mix in the butter, a little at a time.

If mixing by hand, pour the yeast liquid and eggs
into the flour and mix with your fingertips to make a
sticky dough. Then, pulling the dough up from the
work surface and slapping it back down again, work
the dough until it is no longer sticky, and very elastic.
Gradually work in the butter. Put the dough into a

clean, lightly floured, bowl. Cover the bowl with plastic film and refrigerate for at least 5 hours, or overnight, to allow the dough to rise slowly; it should tre-
ble in size.

Butter a long loaf tin, about 30 by 11 by 7.5 cm (12
by 4 1/2 by 3 inches). Turn the risen dough on to a
floured work surface and knead it until smooth—
about 1 minute. Divide it into three equal pieces. Roll
each piece into a long strand, a little longer than the
loaf tin. Place the three strands side by side on the
work surface. Starting in the centre, plait the three
strands together, working towards yourself. Turn the
dough round and plait the other end.

Place the plait in the tin. Cover the tin loosely with
plastic film and allow the dough to rise, at room temperature, to the top of the tin—1 to 1 1/4 hours.
Preheat the oven to 220°C (425°F or Mark 7).

When the dough has risen, stir the milk and remaining sugar together until the sugar dissolves, then
brush this glaze evenly over the top of the loaf. Bake
for 10 minutes, then reduce the heat to 190°C (375°F
or Mark 5), and continue baking for 25 to 30 minutes,
until the loaf is golden-brown and sounds hollow
when tapped on the base. Turn the loaf on to a wire
rack to cool.

EDITOR'S NOTE: To make individual brioches, divide the
dough into 14 equal pieces after the first rising. Cut a
quarter off each piece and shape both large and small
pieces into balls. Place the large balls in 9 cm (3 1/2 inch)
brioche moulds with the small balls on top. Leave to rise for
about 30 minutes. Glaze, then bake for 15 to 20 minutes.

Potato Griddle Cakes with Apple-Mustard Compote

Serves 8

Working time: about 45 minutes
Total time: about 1 hour and 10 minutes
Calories 205, Protein 3g, Cholesterol 40mg, Total fat 4g,
Saturated fat 2g, Sodium 160mg

1	potato (about 250g/¹/₂ lb), peeled and diced
1	egg, separated, plus 1 egg white
1 tsp	caster sugar
¹/₄ tsp	salt
¹/₈ tsp	grated nutmeg
75 g/2¹/₂ oz	plain flour

Apple-mustard compote

6	firm, tart apples that will hold their shape when cooked, quartered, cored, peeled and cut into eighths
6 tbsp	sugar
6 tbsp	unsweetened apple juice
30 g/1 oz	unsalted butter
40 g/1¹/₄ oz	sultanas
1	lemon, grated rind and juice
¹/₂ tsp	ground cinnamon
2 tbsp	grainy mustard

Put the diced potato into a saucepan and cover it with water. Bring the water to the boil, then reduce the heat, and simmer the potato until it is soft—10 to 15 minutes.

While the potato is cooking, prepare the apple-mustard compote. Put the apples, sugar, apple juice, but-ter, sultanas, lemon rind and lemon juice into a heavy frying pan over medium-high heat. Cook the mixture, stirring frequently, until the apples are heated through and tender—about 5 minutes. Stir in the cinnamon and mustard, and keep the compote warm while you make the griddle cakes. (If you like, you can make the compote a day ahead and reheat it.)

Drain the cooked potato, reserving ¹/₄ litre (8 fl oz) of the cooking liquid. Put the potato into a bowl and mash it with a potato masher or a fork until it is smooth; alternatively, work the potato through a sieve. Stir in the reserved cooking liquid and let the mashed potato cool to lukewarm.

Stir the egg yolk, sugar, salt and nutmeg into the mashed potato. Sift in the flour and stir the mixture just until it is blended.

Put the egg whites into a bowl and beat them until they form soft peaks. Stir about a quarter of the egg whites into the potato mixture and then gently fold in the remaining egg whites.

Heat a large griddle or frying pan over medium heat until a few drops of cold water dance when sprinkled on the surface. Spoon about 4 tablespoons of the bat-ter at a time on to the griddle or pan and use the back of the spoon to spread the batter into rounds. Cook the griddle cakes until they are covered with bubbles and the undersides are golden—1 to 3 minutes. Flip the cakes and cook them until the second sides are lightly browned—about 1 minute more. Transfer the cakes to a platter and keep them warm while you cook the remaining batter. Serve the griddle cakes im-mediately with the apple-mustard compote.

Orange, Grapefruit
and Honeydew Melon with Port

Serves 8
Working (and total) time: about 40 minutes
Calories 120, Protein 1g, Cholesterol 0mg, Total fat 0g,
Saturated fat 0g, Sodium 20mg

1	*grapefruit, preferably pink*
2	*oranges*
12.5 cl/4 fl oz	*ruby port or Madeira*
12.5 cl/4 fl oz	*fresh orange juice*
2 tbsp	*light or dark brown sugar*
1	*honeydew melon, seeded and peeled, the flesh cut into eight wedges and chilled*

Peel and segment the grapefruit and the oranges as demonstrated below, reserving the juices. Strain the juices into a small saucepan. Put the fruit in a bowl and refrigerate it while you make the sauce.

Add the port or Madeira, the 12.5 cl (4 fl oz) of orange juice and the sugar to the citrus juices in the saucepan, and bring the mixture to the boil. Reduce the heat to medium and simmer the liquid until it is reduced to about 12.5 cl (4 fl oz)—about 25 minutes. Let the sauce cool, then stir it into the fruit in the bowl.

Meanwhile, cut one wedge of honeydew melon in half crosswise, then into thin slices. Spread the slices in the shape of a fan on a chilled individual serving plate. Repeat the process with the remaining wedges. Spoon the citrus segments and the sauce over the melon fans and serve them at once.

Orange French Toast

Serves 8

Working time: about 30 minutes
Total time: about 45 minutes
Calories 385, Protein 10g, Cholesterol 105mg, Total fat
6g, Saturated fat 1g, Sodium 375mg

25 g/³/₄ oz	*sliced almonds*
1	*loaf (about 500 g/1 lb) unsliced day-old dense white or wholemeal bread, ends trimmed*
3	*eggs, plus 3 egg whites*
45 g/¹/₄ oz	*caster sugar*
¹/₄ tsp	*salt*
1	*orange, grated rind only*
1 tsp	*pure vanilla extract*
35 cl/12 fl oz	*fresh orange juice*
Orange syrup	
175 g/6 oz	*light brown sugar*
175 g/6 oz	*frozen orange juice concentrate*

Preheat the oven to 190°C (375°F or Mark 5). In a small, heavy frying pan set over medium heat, toast the almonds, stirring constantly, until they are golden-brown—about 5 minutes. Remove the almonds from the pan and set them aside.

Cut the bread into 16 slices about 1 cm (¹/₂ in) thick. In a shallow dish, whisk together the eggs, egg whites, caster sugar, salt, orange rind and vanilla extract, then stir in the fresh orange juice.

Dip the bread slices into the juice mixture, turning them once or twice until they are thoroughly soaked with the liquid; transfer the slices to a large plate or baking sheet as you work. After all the slices have been soaked, dribble any remaining liquid over them.

Heat a large griddle or frying pan over medium heat until a few drops of cold water dance when sprinkled on the surface. Cook the slices until the undersides are golden—about 3 minutes. Turn the slices and cook them until the second sides are lightly browned—2 to 3 minutes more. Transfer the French toast to a clean baking sheet. Brown the remaining slices and transfer them to the baking sheet, too. Bake the French toast until it is cooked through and has puffed up—about 10 minutes.

While the toast is baking, make the orange syrup. Pour ¹/₄ litre (8 fl oz) of water into a small saucepan and stir in the brown sugar; bring the liquid to the boil. Reduce the heat to medium low and simmer the mixture to dissolve the sugar—about 1 minute. Add the orange juice concentrate and cook the syrup, stirring, until it is heated through—about 1 minute more. Pour the syrup into a pitcher.

Divide the French toast among eight warmed plates and sprinkle each serving with some toasted almonds. Pass the syrup separately.

Prunes with Orange, Pineapple and Kiwi Fruit

Serves 6
Working (and total) time: about 30 minutes
Calories 90, Protein 1g, Cholesterol 0mg, Total fat 0g,
Saturated fat 0g, Sodium 2mg

500 g/1 lb	*dried stoned prunes, quartered*
1½ tsp	*cornflour*
6 tbsp	*fresh orange juice*
3 tbsp	*honey*
½ tsp	*pure vanilla extract*
1	*orange*
150 g/5 oz	*fresh pineapple, cut into 2.5 cm (1 inch) wedges*
1	*kiwi fruit, halved and cut into 12 pieces (six pieces per half)*

Put the prunes and 60 cl (1 pint) of hot water into a bowl. Cover the bowl and microwave it on high until the water simmers—about 4 minutes. Remove the bowl from the oven and let the prunes stand, covered, for about 10 minutes.

Meanwhile, combine the cornflour and the fresh orange juice in a bowl, then stir in the honey and the vanilla extract. Cook the mixture on high until it thickens—about 2 minutes.

Using a sharp, stainless-steel knife, cut off both ends of the orange. Stand the orange on end and cut away vertical strips of the peel and pith. Slice the orange into 5 mm (¼ inch) thick rounds. Cut the rounds in half.

Drain the prunes and put them into a bowl with the orange, pineapple and kiwi fruit. Pour the honey mixture over the fruits and stir them together gently. Microwave the fruit mixture on high for 1½ minutes to heat it through. Serve the fruit warm.

Puffy Fruit Omelette

Serves 4 as a main dish
Working (and total) time: about 40 minutes
Calories 200, Protein 10g, Cholesterol 140mg, Total fat
5g, Saturated fat 1g, Sodium 250mg

2	*eggs, separated, plus 2 egg whites*
2 tbsp	*plain flour*
¹/₂ tsp	*baking powder*
¹/₈ tsp	*salt*
12.5 cl/4 fl oz	*semi-skimmed milk*
15 g/¹/₂ oz	*caster sugar*
1 tsp	*safflower oil*
1	*red eating apple, quartered, cored and cut into 1 cm (¹/₂ inch) pieces*
1	*pear, quartered, cored and cut into 1 cm (¹/₂ inch) pieces*
1 tsp	*fresh lemon juice*
¹/₄ tsp	*ground cinnamon*
2 tbsp	*raspberry jam*
2 tbsp	*unsweetened apple juice*

Preheat the oven to 230°C (450°F or Mark 8). In a bowl, whisk together the egg yolks, flour, baking powder, salt and 3 tablespoons of the milk until the mixture is well blended—5 to 7 minutes. Whisk in the remaining milk.

In another bowl, beat the egg whites with 3 teaspoons of the sugar until they form soft peaks. Stir half of the whites into the yolk mixture and then gently fold in the remaining whites just until the mixture is blended; do not overmix. Set the egg mixture aside.

Heat the oil in a large, shallow fireproof casserole over medium-high heat. Add the apple and the pear, the remaining sugar, the lemon juice and the cinnamon and cook the fruit, stirring frequently, until it is tender—about 5 minutes. Remove the casserole from the heat and pour the egg mixture over the fruit; smooth the top of the mixture with a spatula. Place the casserole in the oven and bake the omelette until the top is golden-brown—10 to 15 minutes.

While the omelette is baking, mix together the raspberry jam and the unsweetened apple juice in a small dish. When the omelette is ready, dribble this syrup over it, slice it into quarters and serve immediately.

Raspberry Frappé

Makes 6 servings
Working time: about 20 minutes
Total time: about 1 hour and 45 minutes (includes chilling)
Calories 130, Protein 3g, Cholesterol 4mg, Total fat 1g,
Saturated fat 1g, Sodium 30mg

³/₄ litre/1¹/₄ pints	*fresh orange juice*
2 tbsp	*instant tapioca*
2 tbsp	*sugar, if you are using fresh raspberries*
250 g/8 oz	*fresh or frozen raspberries*
30 cl/¹/₂ pint	*semi-skimmed milk*

Put the orange juice into a non-reactive saucepan; stir in the tapioca and the sugar, if you are using it, and let the mixture stand for 5 minutes. Bring the liquid to the boil, stirring constantly. Remove the pan from the heat and let the mixture cool completely.

Add the raspberries and purée the mixture, one half at a time, in a blender or a food processor. Strain each batch through a fine sieve. Cover the purée with plastic film and chill it for at least 1 hour, then whisk in the milk. If you like, serve the frappé in chilled glasses.

Sliced Apples on Toast

Serves 6
Working time: about 30 minutes
Total time: about 35 minutes
Calories 190, Protein 3g, Cholesterol 10mg, Total fat 5g,
Saturated fat 3g, Sodium 120mg

30 g/1 oz	unsalted butter
5	apples, peeled, halved, cored and thinly sliced
3 tbsp	fresh lemon juice
3 tbsp	maple syrup
6	slices wholemeal bread, toasted
1 tbsp	sugar

Preheat the oven to 240°C (475°F or Mark 9).

Melt the butter in a large, non-stick frying pan over medium heat. Add the apple slices, lemon juice and maple syrup and cook the mixture until the apples are soft—about 5 minutes.

Drain the cooking liquid from the apples into a bowl and set it aside. Allow the apples to cool slightly. Divide the apples equally among the pieces of toast, overlapping the apple slices slightly. Sprinkle each piece of apple toast with some of the sugar.

Bake the apple toast until the apple slices are hot and the bread is very crisp—about 5 minutes. Dribble some of the reserved cooking liquid over each apple toast and serve hot.

Tangerine Marmalade

Makes 250 g (8 oz)
Working time: about 10 minutes
Total time: about 2 hours and 30 minutes (includes cooling)
Per tablespoon: Calories 55, Protein 0g, Cholesterol 0mg,
Total fat 0g, Saturated fat 0g, Sodium 0mg

250 g/8 oz *tangerines (about three)*
1/8 tsp *pure vanilla extract*
150g/5 oz *sugar*

Remove the peel from the tangerines and chop it finely. Put the chopped peel into a measuring jug. Squeeze the tangerines and strain the juice into the measuring jug; add the vanilla extract and stir well. If necessary, add enough water to measure 1/4 litre (8 fl oz).

Pour the tangerine mixture into a bowl and microwave it, uncovered, on high for 5 minutes. Stir in the sugar and microwave the bowl on high for 5 minutes more. Stir the mixture and then microwave it for 3 minutes more. Test the marmalade for consistency by dropping a spoonful of it on to a chilled plate. Let the marmalade cool for 1 minute and then push it gently with your finger tip; it should wrinkle slightly as you push it. If the marmalade fails to wrinkle, microwave it for up to 1 minute more and then test it again; but be very careful not to overcook the marmalade or it will become too thick.

Let the marmalade cool to room temperature before serving it—about 2 hours. The marmalade can be stored in the refrigerator for up to two weeks.

EDITOR'S NOTE: If the marmalade thickens too much during refrigeration, you can thin it by microwaving it, uncovered, on high for 1 minute. Stir in 2 tablespoons of water and microwave it on high for 2 minutes more; then allow it to cool.

Seedless Cranberry Jam

Makes 600 g (1 1/4 lb)
Working time: about 10 minutes
Total time: about 8 hours (includes chilling)
Per tablespoon: Calories 25, Protein 0g, Cholesterol 0mg
Total fat 0g, Saturated fat 0g, Sodium 0mg

350 g/12 oz *cranberries, picked over*
150 g/5 oz *sugar*
1 tbsp *liquid pectin*

Put the cranberries into a 2 litre (3 1/2 pint) glass bowl with 1/4 litre (8 fl oz) of water and microwave them on high, uncovered, for 6 minutes.

Work the cranberries through a sieve set over a bowl and discard the contents of the sieve. Add the sugar to the bowl and stir the mixture. Microwave the cranberry mixture on high for 8 minutes, stirring half way through the cooking time. Remove the bowl from the oven, stir in the pectin, and let the jam cool.

Spoon the jam into a jar, and cover and chill it overnight. Cranberry jam can be kept for up to 2 weeks covered and stored in the refrigerator.

Wheat Berry Muffins

Makes 12 muffins

Working time: about 20 minutes

Total time: about 2 hours

Per muffin: Calories 210, Protein 7g, Cholesterol 45mg,
Total fat 4g, Saturated fat 1g, Sodium 210mg

100 g/3½ oz	*wheat berries*
175 g/6 oz	*plain flour*
125 g/4 oz	*wholemeal flour*
60 g/2 oz	*dried skimmed milk*
1 tsp	*baking powder*
1 tsp	*bicarbonate of soda*
½ tsp	*ground cinnamon*
¼ tsp	*salt*
2	*eggs*
90 g/3 oz	*honey*
2 tbsp	*safflower oil*
35 cl/12 fl oz	*buttermilk*
75 g/2½ oz	*raisins*

Bring ¼ litre (8 fl oz) of water to the boil in a saucepan and then add the wheat berries. Reduce the heat to low, cover the pan and simmer the kernels until they are tender—1½ to 2 hours. If the wheat berries absorb all the water before they finish cooking, pour in more water, 4 tablespoons at a time, to keep them from burning. Drain them and set them aside.

Preheat the oven to 190°C (375°F or Mark 5). Lightly oil 12 cups in a muffin tin or deep bun tin. Sift together the two flours, the dried milk, baking powder, bicarbonate of soda, cinnamon and salt in a bowl. In another bowl, mix the eggs with the honey and the oil and stir in the buttermilk. Combine the egg mixture with the flour mixture and stir just until they are blended; do not overmix. Fold in the wheat berries and raisins.

Spoon the batter into the cups in the tin, filling each one no more than two-thirds full. Bake the muffins until they are golden-brown—16 to 18 minutes. Serve the muffins immediately.